This book is dedicated to **Kerry Simpson,** my wife**,** my best friend, my confidant, my lover, my rock, my absolute everything. Without a doubt my story wouldn't have ended up the way it has, and I might not have even been around to write it. Kerry, I love you!

Acknowledgements

Firstly, to my children, Oliver, Joshua and Maia, I know the two of you that are currently old enough to understand roll your eyes when I talk about neurodiversity or my journey. However, I am doing this for you and your future families. I aspire to leave this world a better place than I found it, and I am confident that one day you will appreciate this book and cherish it. To little Maia, currently three and non-verbal, save for her singing, I hope to effect change that will impact you. My wish is to enable you to showcase your amazing strengths to the world and forge a path for you to achieve your fullest potential. You are all amazing, never let anyone tell you any different and ALWAYS be proud to be yourselves.

Next I have to thank my two best friends, Paul Mason (AKA Duuuude!) and Steve Cook (AKA Bunter), these guys have always been there for me and, as I have developed personally, I have been there to return the favour, which has given me great satisfaction.. Thanks guys!

I would also like to thank my teacher from years gone by Jane Cooper. I won't spoil the story but Jane has played a massive part in my journey including marking my homework one more time by proofreading this book, thank you Jane, former teacher and now dear friend.

I would also like to thank everyone I have encountered on my journey and I mean everyone, good or bad experiences, you have all taught me something about myself and the world around me, thank you for your lessons. Some of you have possibly saved my life without even knowing it. Others made me want to take my life but I hold no grudges, just lessons learnt.

Disclaimer and Content Warning

A Note on Privacy and Perspective

To safeguard the privacy of individuals and businesses mentioned in this memoir, the names of the majority of people, workplaces, and companies have been changed or redacted. Where real names are used (e.g., historical figures, certain teachers, or well-known public figures), it is with permission or because they have entered the public domain. This book is a retelling of personal events and memory, and any perceived resemblance to living or deceased persons is unintentional.

I hold absolutely **no grudges** against anyone I have ever worked with or for. Any difficult interactions described reflect a period of immense personal struggle and a lack of mutual understanding regarding neurodiversity. I acknowledge that when I point a finger, there are always three pointing back, and that every manager and colleague is on their own journey of personal development and dealing with their own life circumstances.

Content Warning

This book discusses periods of severe **mental health crisis**, including **depression** and **suicidal ideation**.

If reading this content brings up overwhelming emotion or crisis, please seek immediate help. You will find a comprehensive list of **emergency contacts and mental health resources** in the dedicated section at the back of this book (**Part 2 - Chapter 5 - Resources and Next Steps**).

Introduction

It's 05:33 am. I was awoken over an hour ago when our 9-month-old daughter, Maia, woke up for a bottle. I can't get to sleep. My brain is engaged, and already, hundreds of thoughts are racing through my mind, many of which revolve around **neurodiversity** and how I can help others.

The idea of writing this book has always been there. So many times, I wrote chapters in my head, content that I knew others on a similar journey would find helpful. Still, the thoughts would come and go, disappearing into the ether. I often feel empowered, convinced this is the right thing to do, but then the self-doubt creeps in. *What will others think of my struggles? Will it ruin my career? Will anyone actually care what I have to say?*

However, **I have decided right now that I am going to do this.** This journey, my need to go back in time to understand my life so far, needs to be captured. (EDIT: It actually took 3 years to finish the book, yet I wrote most of it in a month, the hold up was mistakenly thinking about what others would think about it.)

My story needs to be captured for several reasons. We need people to lead the way. For years, I sat alone in the darkness, convinced it was just me. My mental health was in a terrible place; so many times, I have been to the edge of darkness, looking down at the black hole of emptiness. I do not want others to feel that loneliness. I want people to read about my journey and realise they can stop beating themselves up constantly, day after day, night after night, and that they are not the problem.

This book is my mission to educate others, to open people's minds, and to help them discover what those around them may be going through daily. It will provide the insights needed to become better **leaders** of people, be that as a **CEO**, a **teacher**, or a **parent**, creating a win-win situation for everyone.

Finally, on a selfish note, this is therapy. After all those years of suffering, personal torture, self-beating, and wanting to be someone else, I can finally release the pressure and be at peace with myself.

So why **'Binman to Boardroom'**? Well, it's my journey, one I'm still on and one I hope to continue. Around ten years ago, I metamorphosed, emerging from that cocoon of darkness into a world of light and self-discovery. I had spent nine years driving a dustcart. I had come to believe the lie that this was my lot, a life of being talked down to and treated like the dirt on someone's shoe. In fact, as I started to emerge, my manager at the time said, **"You made a fantastic impression of being thick all of those years."** Thanks, Martin!

And the Boardroom part? I'm getting there. I am now a **Chartered Management Accountant**, working for a global automotive manufacturer and advising its executive leadership. (EDIT: As I prepare to publish this book I have started not one, but two businesses. A Chartered Accountancy Practice, that I plan to grow and enable others to have the journey I've had. Albeit easier. Also I am attempting to make a business out of helping others, talking about my journey, how I got there and how they can too and trying to inspire change in the world for the good of others)

I'd now like to take you on a journey, one of massive self-discovery and social mobility, one of torture and pain, bullying, loneliness, and some very dark moments, through to moments where I felt so proud and achieved things beyond my wildest dreams. I want to share how I changed from being totally ignorant and uneducated about **neurodiversity** to learning about it through my son's diagnosis of **Autism** and finally being diagnosed myself.

Part 1 - The Journey from Binman To Boardroom

Chapter 1 - My Journey - First Memories

This is where I get to share my amazing journey with you. Well, from the outside, it all seems amazing. However, it's been grueling. There have been dark times; there have been times I have nearly given up, there have been times I felt so tired that I didn't feel I could carry on. I am keen to show both sides. Too often today, with social media, we see just the shiny good stuff and the success, and that is damaging to people. More people need to share not just the tip of the iceberg, but also the foundations—the largest part of the iceberg sat under the water. That's the failure, the anxiety, the dedication and hard work. That's the sacrifice, the disappointment, criticism, and rejection. That's where you build resilience and become the person strong enough to grow your iceberg out of the water and show your glorious success.

You will also learn that, even though people see success, for many—especially those that are **neurodivergent**—what goes on behind the scenes is still **a personal beating** that we need to do better, and we still aren't good enough. You will learn, though, that this is actually a trait that can help get you to your destination; you just need to manage it carefully.

I'm also keen to show my vulnerability and share some of my personal journey. This is because it is part of the makeup of who we are as individuals. It's not just our genes; our personality is made up from the experiences we have in life, both personally and professionally. People tell me it's brave to do this. I don't feel brave; I just feel, as a good human, I need to do this to help others. I have felt so desperately lonely on my journey and through my struggles. I want to be that person that is there with you—someone that can let you know you are not alone in your struggles, there are others that suffer and struggle, and that, with persistence, you too can truly change your life.

I was born in the late 1970s in Cambridgeshire.

Let's cast back to Monday, September 6th, 1982, in the small fenland village of Warboys. This was the day my life was about to change forever: my first day at school! I remember it as if it was yesterday, walking along holding my Mum's hand, trying not to step on the gaps and cracks in the paving. Being in my own world was good; it helped me as I was really nervous. On the way we called for my best friend Toby. We knocked on the door; Toby wasn't ready. His Mum called up telling him to make sure he'd washed behind his ears. I don't know why I remember that bit, but it's just the clearest bit of the whole day! I don't remember the rest of that day; I'm guessing it was the overwhelm of everything going on, and I just switched off.

To be honest, during my first school years, up until age nine, I only have a few memories. It's funny how the brain works, isn't it? I remember Toby being called and can visualise that walk to school, but the next 4 years? Hardly a thing! What I do remember is being stood in the corner with my hands on my head—that was the punishment back then for being naughty. In fact, I had it good; I'll speak later about my best friend Paul. He was treated terribly at school. It turns out his behaviour was due to undiagnosed dyslexia! There are a few other things I remember. I remember lying on my back in the playground, covering my ears and kicking my legs with a gang of kids around me trying to fight me. I remember being alone in the playground trying to fit in; I just never did.

The World of Order and Precision

I have good memories too. In Warboys there was a small, rectangular village pond in the centre of the village between a fork in the road. It had a low concrete fence around it, and around the perimeter of that was grass, trees, and benches. It was known as Warboys Weir and is mentioned in the Domesday Book in 1086; it was there as far back as medieval times. It's a mysterious place with a rich history of witches being thrown in there to test their guilt: if they floated, they were guilty, and if they sank, they were innocent. I'm not quite sure they thought that through!

The Weir was the start of a huge obsession for me that would take over my every thought. One still summer day, with glorious blue skies, my Dad took me there with a fishing rod. I loved it: it was quiet, it was still. We sat there looking at the mirror-like surface of the pond with the little day-glo orange tipped float just breaking the surface next to the lily pads. It was my heaven!

The float dipped under, and my Dad excitedly told me to lift the rod. I lifted it and felt the pull of a fish. I was so excited, my face beaming. We lifted the rod up, and my Dad grabbed the fish. It was a shimmering golden Rudd with beautiful, perfect scales along its flank and deep, blood-red fins. It was like a bar of gold, a thing of beauty. I knelt down as my Dad gently lowered it back into the water, and we watched it swim away, back to its refuge under the lilies. That was it: I had found my passion! Despite my Dad wanting me to be into football, I just had little interest. From that day on, fishing would be everything to me!

My First Meltdowns and Sensory Struggles

It wasn't all sunshine and fishing though. It was back in this house in Warboys that I can remember what I now know as a **meltdown**. I remember barricading myself in my bedroom and crying my eyes out on many occasions. I can't recall why, to be honest. I also remember the punishment for being naughty; it was a slipper or a belt I was hit with, and if I struggled, that would end up around my head. I don't blame my Dad. I love my Dad to bits, and later in life we have become very close due to the struggles we have both shared. I don't blame him as this was just about normal back then. It's how poor behaviour was treated: not trying to understand why and helping to deal with the root cause—it was just punishment and forced change. It's how the world worked back then. Before that, it was worse: children were even beaten at school for being left handed and made to write with their right hand. One thing I have learnt to deal with over the years is that you cannot change the past and you cannot leave your mind in the past; you have to learn to move on. This is really hard, but it can be done.

This is where I also have my first memories of wanting to know how things worked. I took everything apart with my Dad's tools when he wasn't around. In fact, that's probably what I got told off for most. I remember my younger sister having a little bike that looked like a Vespa-style scooter. It had stabilisers and was a pale yellow colour with a white fairing. It was a bike, but it looked like a motorised scooter. It fascinated me how it was made. It obsessed me looking at it, so I had to do it. I took it apart to find out how it was made. I was probably around 7 or 8 at the time! I even took apart walkmans and radios. I remember using the electric motors to make little winches and tow my toy cars!

Turning to toys, I had a different way of playing with my toys. I loved model cars, and I would line them up all around the house in colour order, going through the different colours and shades from light to dark. I wouldn't so much play with them. I just loved having them all in order. I can still picture today my deep burgundy Jaguar XJ6, my black Ford Mustang Cobra 2 with yellow stripes up the middle. One model I wasn't allowed though was my Dad's bright red E-Type Jaguar, his dream car.

The other memory that I still find so satisfying is art sets, those sets you would get for Christmas: a big plastic case with a spectrum of coloured pencils all in a row like soldiers, in colour order of the spectrum, and all the points the same size and length. I can still smell these art sets, the felt-tips and crayons, if I close my eyes. The order of these sets just gave me so much joy; I loved things in order. In fact, so much so, that many of these sets were unused as I didn't want the coloured pencils to end up at different lengths. I needed them to stay perfect; that would give me more joy than actually using them. I still get a huge satisfaction from sets of things now. I love order and structure. It's actually come to cost me a fair bit of money over my lifetime so far; even my fishing floats are in sets, and I have a desire to have the full range in different sizes, all in order of course!

Another difference I had, looking back, was how fussy I was as an eater. I didn't like things mixed together; I liked them separate on the plate. I would save the best bit to last, eating things separately in order of enjoyment. I also had an issue with textures, and that was quite limiting. I couldn't eat bananas for example, and today, despite liking the taste, I still cannot stand bananas! They make me go all on edge; you know, the sort of feeling you might get if someone scrapes their nails along a chalkboard. I cook a fantastic banana and walnut loaf but even cringe peeling them to make it.

I remember my diet being quite limited. The only meats I would eat were sausages or chicken breast. I wouldn't eat tomatoes or eggs due to texture. My favourite meal was sausage, mashed potato, cabbage, carrots, and gravy! I also remember once eating an orange ice lolly and being put off by the texture as I bit into it; I can still visualise it.

The Penguin Boy

Another thing that happened to me in these years was an accident. I can't remember it, but it's something I was told about and something I have mentioned many times since. At around the age of four, my Dad was building a conservatory. It wasn't UPVC like you see now, but a kit of prefabricated wooden windows and a plastic corrugated roof. Apparently, my Dad left a piece of wood on the ground with a nail sticking out of it, and I stood on it; it went straight through my left foot! I'll talk later about how I was bullied for the way I walk for many years. At school, I was often called 'penguin boy' due to my odd gait, and people still comment occasionally now.

For many years I blamed it on this incident. It wasn't until I started to learn about **Autism** and was diagnosed that I learnt that many people that are Autistic have a changed gait. Much of this is caused by walking on tiptoes as they learn to walk. Research shows that this is due to a dysfunctional vestibular system; it is the vestibular system that provides our brains with feedback on our bodies position and motion. Our daughter walks on her tiptoes too, and I have also witnessed many people in the work environment that have turned out 'pigeon toes' and an odd gait alongside many Autistic traits. Many of these people are undiagnosed. I can't diagnose people, but it is quite fascinating seeing it all piece together with the knowledge I have built over the years.

Chapter 2 - My Journey - Things Get Dark

At the age of **nine**, a big change came along in my life. My Dad had recently started a business delivering soft drinks from door to door and had started to expand into eggs, potatoes, crisps and sweets. It was back when fizzy pop was sold in glass bottles which you would return for a refund and would be reused. It always amazes me how we have gone backwards. Dad's business model would have been great now, as people want more recycling and the world needs to rid itself of single-use plastics. Furthermore, the growth in home delivery for groceries has grown extensively, with a now estimated 37.4% of the UK population having their groceries delivered to their homes.

Dad worked extremely long hours and built his business from investing some redundancy money he received from Perkins Engines in Peterborough, where he was a rectification engineer for marine, tank and agricultural engines. I don't remember spending much time with my Dad over these years while he built the business. It got bigger and bigger, and eventually he needed to not only upgrade the **second-hand** Ford Transit pickup he had but also to get a proper premises, as he was having a full HGV lorry load of soft drinks delivered from the manufacturer every week along with crates of eggs and sacks of potatoes from local farms. Dad had a small industrial unit but wanted a place where he could keep everything together, and so looked to move us from our mid-terraced housing association home to a bigger place with room for his business.

The Move to Ramsey St Marys

We moved into a detached cottage in Ramsey St Marys in Cambridgeshire, a very small village. The cottage was built in the 1500s and had been modernised with the downstairs ceiling height increased, meaning that the upstairs window sills were just around 30cm off of the floor, and the bedroom ceilings were sloped as they now encroached into what was once the loft space. The great thing about this home was that it had three-quarters of an acre of garden—about the size of **eight** tennis courts! It also had a large gravel drive going around to the rear of the house, a large concrete hard standing area, perfect for crates of drinks, a double garage, **three brick-built** sheds and a very large wooden shed.

It sounds exciting, and for a while it was, but I was lonely. I found it hard to make friends; I certainly wasn't in the cool gang. I just felt different, and as much as I tried, I just didn't really fit in. I spent most of my time at home. There weren't many TV channels back then—just three—no internet, and no DVDs or CDs; it was VHS videos and Vinyl. Wow, I sound old, but really, I'm not!

My Dad was rarely home, working from early morning to late evenings and even weekends. My Mum didn't really do much with us, apart from a bit of cooking. I was always getting told off as I would take things apart or do something or other wrong. A lot of the time my sister would set me up to get into trouble; Mum always took her side.

Fishing: My Obsession and My Peace

Fishing was what I started to live for. Dad had found a local fishing club for me, and two guys called Keith and 'Ginger' were the men that volunteered to run junior matches regularly on a Sunday. My Dad would often drop me off there, and I would spend five hours fishing in a competition against around 20 other kids. Ginger was amazing; such a nice, patient guy. He used to lend me his kit as I didn't have much, and he would spend hours teaching me, occasionally going off down the bank of the fen drain to check on the others. Ginger had so much time for me; he was such a lovely guy!

I remember one of the first times he left me to wander off and check the others. It was on what was known as the 'Forty Foot Drain'. This was a fairly straight, river-like drainage channel, and part of Sir Cornelius Vermuyden's 'Great Drainage Scheme.' It was **hand-dug** in the 1600s to drain the water from the fenlands of Cambridgeshire to allow for agriculture. I remember sitting on the black plastic 'Daiwa seatbox' watching the rod tip like nothing else mattered in the world, waiting for a fish to grab the bait and start the tip quivering. I remember the excitement as it started to move backwards and forwards and whip around into a distinct bend. I started to wind. It felt massive. I was shaking with excitement and shouted, "Ginger, I've caught a whopper!" Ginger ran back and helped me land the fish. It wasn't quite the amazing golden Rudd I'd caught in Warboys, but a horrid, slimy Eel—yuk! I was no way going near that slimy, snake-like creature; it scared me! I still get the shivers now when it comes to Eels!

Fishing though became my obsession. It had everything I loved: peace and quiet, no annoying sister to get me into trouble, no nagging Mum, no one bullying me. There was a complete stillness. I felt calm in and around nature—well, apart from those slimy Eels, the spiky Perch and the Pike, yes, they had teeth! With a large umbrella I'd even happily sit there all day in the rain; I loved it. The other thing I loved was my fishing kit. When I wasn't fishing I would sit and admire my kit. I had a small wooden tackle box by this time, a present from my Uncle Derek, another very keen fisherman. It was varnished and had brass latches holding together two opening compartments. One side had slotted foam strips where my floats were housed, of course, in size and colour order with the amazing fluorescent yellow and orange tips! The other side had deeper compartments, lined with a green velvet-type material, and housed my weights, hook, line and float rubbers etc. It was always spick and span. I could sit for hours just in awe of the collection of kit I was starting to build; it gave me great pleasure.

The Closed Season and The Darkness

There was something that would stop this enjoyment though: the closed season. Back then in the UK all coarse fishing was banned between March 15th and June 15th inclusive. It was these months that were the darkest of my life as a child. I craved the respite of fishing, I missed it dearly and I started to feel very sad when I couldn't go. Fishing excited me so much that I struggled to sleep the night before a fishing trip. By the time I was 10, fishing was all I would talk about. It was an absolute obsession, and not being able to go used to put me in a very dark place. It would be during these times that I started to get the signs of what I now know to be depression.

The worst I remember was locking myself in one of the many outbuildings we had with my dog Cindy. She was my friend, a lovely

Jack Russell and Corgi crossbreed. We welcomed Cindy to our family just before I was born. My Mum had several miscarriages before successfully giving birth to me and therefore was told to bed rest for the whole of the pregnancy. My Dad brought Cindy to keep my Mum company at home. I remember sitting there with Cindy, crying my eyes out. I felt sad, I just didn't know why, I just couldn't explain it. It seemed the closed fishing season would be full of these dark times. It was like there was nothing in my life worth doing. I had no energy. It was like someone had turned off the lights.

A Farm Island and My First Sense of Unfairness

I did have one friend through this time, his name was Lynden. Lynden was very much a loner like me and a bit separate from the other kids, although he had a better relationship with them than me, maybe as he had grown up with them. We used to go to his Grandpa's farm. I loved it there. I would travel in the back of an old blue Renault van, just sat on the floor, no seats. There would just be some hay and cattle feed, I can still visualise and smell it now, such great memories. I particularly liked it that the farm was on the other side of the drainage channel I used to fish in and you had to cross a bridge to get to it; it was like it was on its own giant island. There were giant stacks of round hay bales in a big pyramid shape that we would climb up and slide down; it was fantastic. We would also, during the harvesting season, bag the potatoes up for some pocket money and feed the bullocks too. Going out in the tractor was amazing fun and we used to sit in the cab whilst Brian ploughed or sprayed the crops. On the odd occasion Brian would come to our house in the tractor and mow our lawn—yes, it was a huge lawn! I was allowed to drive the big green John Deere tractor around our garden; I loved it.

Secondary School and the Briefcase

School was a challenge. I had trouble there. I don't remember having many real friends apart from Lynden. I used to hang out with some other kids but they would often just make fun of me. Mr Wales was the head teacher at our school; he was also our teacher. The school was tiny with just around 70 children across all the infants and juniors combined. Mr Wales was really strict, and I remember being told off often. I don't really remember anything good about school.

There was one time where my Dad had brought me a second-hand snare drum, drumsticks and a music book from a music store in Peterborough. My Dad had played drums in a band, and I wanted to have a go. It almost became an obsession as I tried to perfect the paradiddle; however, I just didn't quite have the rhythm! I remember once taking my drum sticks to school and trying to practise in the playground. They were taken off me as they were seen as dangerous! I also remember in the music lesson asking Mr Wales if I could play the drum. He agreed. However, I just could not get the beat and timing. He took it off me, told me I was useless, and gave me the triangle—that hurt! I never played the drum Dad bought me again!

In September 1987, it was time to take that big step into secondary school. The only secondary school was about four miles away in the village of Ramsey, and was split into the lower and upper school with the upper school in the old 15th century Ramsey Abbey. My uncle Steve gave me a gift for my first day, a gift that would get me ridiculed from the moment I stepped on the bus: it was a **second-hand, burgundy leather briefcase!** I actually loved it: I felt grown up, and I could line my stationery up in it and keep everything in order. The other kids didn't share the same enthusiasm, and from day one, I was the kid that everyone made fun of. Those dark days began to get darker!

My only small talk in those days was about fishing. By this time, it was my only interest. I did actually represent the school though, and in 1988 was in the team that won the schools' intercounty championships, on the forty foot drain, not far from where I started my match fishing journey with Ginger. It was here I met John Price who became another friend; however, most of the time John was with the other cool kids, and I did feel a little left out. We did have many fishing trips together though, and his lovely Mum, such a warm, kind Irish lady, would take us there in her little Citroen 2CV 'Dolly'. Even in the coldest, wettest days of winter we would go, and we'd come home to warming home-cooked food. Once I spent the day at John's house and we grabbed an inflatable dinghy from John's garage, and John, his brother, and I went to the local brook in the village of Bury. We put the dinghy in the brook and tried to row but went nowhere. It was decided that I would get out and push us! I waded through the water, pushing us for what seemed miles! We then happened upon a small lake. It had a wooden pier that went out into the lake, and the water was crystal clear; it was like a slice of heaven. I just wanted my fishing rod! No doubt we were probably trespassing though! I remember the feeling of being the one having to push. For many, many years, I was always the underdog—the one that had to do the tough work rather than get the enjoyment. I always had the feeling of me being much less than anyone else.

The Burden and the Bright Spot

I remember my first years at secondary school. I did fairly well. The only thing I remember struggling with was keeping up with writing. When we had a lot of writing to do, my hand would cramp with the most terrible pain, and I'd struggle to keep up; it was excruciating! I fairly enjoyed school, now I had got rid of that briefcase! I didn't like PE though or anything physical, and cross country just felt like torture. I wanted to cry, especially when it was so cold that my hands turned blue!

I did start to struggle though with getting up for school. I would be constantly tired and felt drained, and would often miss the bus and spend the day looking at fishing tackle catalogues! It was strange. I would wake up like a spring in the box for fishing, but school just left me zapped. My Mum would pull my covers off of me to get me out of bed and shout constantly at me.

I could also get up OK during the school holidays to go to work with my Dad. I really enjoyed that too! I would deliver the pop and groceries to people's doors with him, eventually doing it on my own so we could get done faster, and had my own leather money satchel and one of those magic wallets that you put notes in, fold it, and they appear under strips of elastic! I loved dealing with the money and would stack the coins and count them at the end of the day to help Dad cash up. Again, I loved the order of the stacks of coins! I even had my own little lockable metal money box for my tips and wages. It was bright blue and had a pull out black plastic tray with different sections for the different coins, and the notes would sit underneath. Christmas time was great; I used to get loads of tips! I do remember in St. Neots one day a lady tried to take advantage, saying I'd

shortchanged her. I knew I hadn't; I knew my money! When I said I would have to get my Dad, she said that it was OK, she got confused!

The Business Crumbles

It was around 1989 that Dad's business started to struggle. Supermarkets were getting more prevalent, and fizzy drinks were sold there cheaper. In December 1988, politician Edwina Curry decimated UK egg sales, reducing them by 60% after announcing that most UK eggs had salmonella! Huge numbers of chickens were slaughtered, and Edwina resigned two weeks later. Added to these impacts, a relative who had started to work for my Dad was found to be selling produce and keeping the money. Also, interest rates had hit almost 15% by this time, encouraging people to find cheaper goods in the supermarkets and driving up running costs of the business, meaning Dad's business was no longer viable.

Chapter 3 - A Whole New World!

May 8th, 1990, 08:45. My life would change massively from this point on! I had just walked into a new school in the town of Wellingborough!

My Dad's business had dissolved. He had moved to Wellingborough and was staying with my Nan whilst working two jobs as a security guard and a shelf stacker. After a few months of him living away, he had secured a rental house for us—a little semi-detached house, right opposite my new school.

School Hell: The Alien

I walked across the road that day, massively anxious and not wanting to go. I was so apprehensive, my belly full of butterflies, that horrible feeling in my stomach. I just wanted to turn around and cross back over the road into the comfort of my bedroom. I found my form room and stood in the queue. "Hi, my name's Mark," said this voice behind me. I turned around. "I like starting fires," he said. I stalled. What should I say to this? "Oh," I replied. "What's your name?" my new friend asked me. "I'm Gavin, I like fishing," was my reply.

This school was different; the kids were certainly not as well behaved. In fact, they were somewhat unruly. I felt anxious, however, that anxiousness soon turned to sickness and a desire to get the hell out of there. I had addressed a female teacher as **Madam**—it's how we addressed teachers at my last school. The whole class laughed at me; I was like some kind of alien, a complete weirdo. It got worse during the day. I wanted to show I was a good kid and wanted to try my best. At every opportunity, I put my hand up to answer questions. **"You're a boffin, shut up,"** said a girl behind me. *What's a boffin?* I thought, as I just sunk into my seat and into myself. Why was I so different? Why was everyone making fun of me? I got through that day, somehow!

My days at that school never got any better. It wasn't just the kids that mocked me but the teachers too. In one lesson, our science teacher decided that, because of my larger figure, I would be a good example of overnutrition, much to the amusement of the rest of the class. Being laughed at was becoming a regular occurrence. I wasn't the kid who would answer back or swear at the teachers. I just went further within myself, sat there holding the tears back and not saying a word. I didn't even want to participate and answer questions for fear of being mocked. They even mocked my monotonous tone, imitating it every time I spoke.

In PE I was called a **couch potato** by my teacher. He told me **I'd amount to nothing**. I was always the last to be picked for teams; no one wanted me on their team—not that fat, greasy-haired loner. Besides, I admit it, I really was useless. I had rubbish coordination. If a ball flew towards me, I would wince, my eyes shut, and duck out of the way. I was terrified of getting hurt, and I certainly couldn't catch very well or kick straight.

My French teacher tore into me one day, calling me a liar when I'd been off for the day for my Grandad's funeral. All of this just made it worse: **the noise, the rushing and pushing** from class to class finding the next lesson, the abuse, the bullying, the shoving. I couldn't even avoid it at break times. I was known as **Penguin Boy** as I walked with a bit of a side-to-side waddle. As I mentioned earlier, I always believed it to be due to standing on a nail as a toddler. Just walking across the field, I would get laughed at.

The Shutdown

My attendance got to an all-time low. It was around 50%, and my GCSEs were looming. I was taken in to see the head of year with my parents and asked what was wrong. I couldn't speak. In fact, I very rarely spoke any more; I was shutting down. My reply was **nothing**. I knew if I spoke up about bullies I would suffer more; I'd heard the chants of **GRASS, GRASS, GRASS** before during fights in the playground. But it was more than that, something I just couldn't explain.

I felt tired. I struggled to get out of bed every morning. It infuriated my Mum. Often I'd get a rude awakening with a **pint of cold water thrown over my head** whilst I was in bed. That was so distressing. Life was just too much! I was taken to the Doctor. The Doctor asked the same questions. “Who’s after you?” “What are you worried about?” “Nothing,” I’d reply. I just had no answer. I just had no energy. I just struggled. I just wanted to sleep all the time. The Doctor carried out blood tests. I hated it; I felt light-headed and almost fainted.

I would stay at home a lot of the time, on my own, the curtains closed, afraid, hoping no one would knock at the door. I wanted to be alone, in the quiet, no sound, no constant whine. I’d look at fishing magazines and fishing tackle catalogues for hours. I remember the covers of every Shakespeare and Daiwa fishing tackle catalogue from those years vividly. It sounds odd to say, but they gave me so much happiness, calm and satisfaction.

The Sanctuary

There was one teacher though, **Mrs Cooper**. She was amazing. She just didn’t get angry with me. As I had missed so many lessons, she would let me go and sit in a little room away from everyone and catch up on my English Literature essays. It was the best part of school. I sat there on my own: a little office, no windows in the door, blinds at the windows, and just a PC and piles of books in there. I found, in this quiet space, I could work so well. No distractions, no worrying about interacting with others, no looking over my shoulder. I could be me. The silence was so calming. It’s here where I did my best work. Mrs Cooper would set me 400-word assignments. I would regularly come back with **800 words** plus. I found that once I started, I just could not stop writing. The words just flowed out, as they are right now typing this book. I loved writing, well, except for the pain in my wrist and my sweating palms! I still get that now and prefer to type: my writing is terrible, and if I write for too long my hand just cramps.

I hated maths too. I just couldn’t get it. Who would have thought I would become an Accountant! There was just so much to take in, my mind just went to mush. I just sat there in a daze. I just couldn’t get my brain to work. My Dad was right, I was an **idiot**. My PE teacher was right, I would amount to **nothing**.

My GCSEs were looming ever nearer. I can’t remember my parents ever talking to me about my GCSE options; I’m not sure they did. I can remember I took Geography, Art, and double Science, as well as the compulsory English and Maths, and not to forget, my absolute favourite, English Literature, that was taken by the lovely Mrs Cooper. I never did a single bit of revision. It wasn't encouraged, and to be honest, school was such a horrid place to be. I just wanted to escape it and get back into my safe place, my fishing magazines in my bedroom.

Dreams Crushed

Fishing was becoming ever more important to me. I loved it. Sitting by a river, visualising what was going on beneath the surface, no noise but the wind in the trees, no one to bother me. It was my heaven. Even in the depths of winter, I would sit there on my tackle box in the snow. I'd even smashed the ice before, just to fish. I was in a local junior team and was starting to win a few matches on Saturdays. All I spoke about was fishing; it totally absorbed me. I spoke about it a lot when I was at school too, to anyone that would listen. Mrs Cooper listened. I told her that I wanted to become a professional fisherman. To me, it was a sport like darts or snooker, even though it didn't include fitness. Mrs Cooper told me that I had to have another plan, that fishing could never be a job. It made me sad; it's all I wanted to do.

I started to think about what I could do if I wasn't a professional fisherman. I thought about how people buy fish in the supermarket (except me, I can't stand eating fish or seafood), and how lake owners would stock fish into their lakes, and I read about fish farming, breeding fish en masse. I read an article in the *Angler's Mail* about a guy called Doctor Bruno Broughton. He was an expert in fish anatomy. He mentioned a college, I think it was near Melton Mowbray, that specialised in fish farming. This was it. I was going to be a professional fisherman, or a fish farmer!

Armed with this knowledge, I went to a careers meeting at school. I was excited; I had a plan. I was going to do something I loved! A fish farmer? The career lady laughed. **"You can't be a fish farmer, don't be silly. Here, have a look at this CITB leaflet. You could work on a building site and learn a trade. You will always have work."** I sank. Surely there must be a way? How do I get to go to college? No one in my family had been to college or university, that was for really extremely intelligent people and rich families. My excitement was crushed. No, that's it then, I was going to be a professional fisherman, just like Ex World Champion Ian Heaps, one of my idols.

I would just live in a deep dark world all week, just waiting for Sunday morning to arrive. I'd be excited trying to get to sleep, knowing I was going fishing the next day. My tackle was well prepared, and my bait was perfected. I ran through my plan in my head, visualising the rig I would use and how it would work in the water, how I would tempt the fish with my loose feed strategy, and how I would win the match. I would wake the next day at 6 am, buzzing and ready to go. Two slices of toast and a cup of tea, get dressed, and I was chomping at the bit to get into the car.

I was starting to win more and more, and at 15 I was starting to fish adult matches, with sometimes up to 300 anglers taking part. I used to fish occasionally against a lad my age called Steve Ringer from Northampton. Eventually, many years later, Steve became World Champion and is one of Europe's greatest anglers, and even has his own fishing bait business!

The Financial Crisis and New Work

Back at home, life was getting rough. We moved into a housing association house. We moved in on Boxing Day one year as Mum was so fed up; it was the best thing we could think of doing. We never had proper carpet in that house for as long as we lived there. It was a dark blue textured offcut in the lounge that finished about 30cm before the skirting boards. Mum and Dad were struggling for money. We had an old Ford Escort. I remember Dad using a bit of an old dog food tin and some filler to fix the body work for an MOT failure. Mum and Dad argued a lot; home wasn't a great place. We didn't even have holidays any more.

Dad worked hard and now had a job as a Traffic Warden. He was Wellingborough's most loved Traffic Warden though. He hated conflict, was, and still is such a soft, laid-back man, and he would go and find people and get them to move rather than give them a ticket. Although I do remember him once coming home shaken up as a woman decided she was going to run him down with her car! Mum eventually got a job at the police station too, as a cook in the canteen. I'd often go there and have my dinner with the police officers, sometimes even a second dinner, food was comforting.

My GCSEs were now about to start. I still wasn't revising. I had no drive. Home life was now also getting stressful, and Mum and Dad didn't really have an interest in my school work. However, I had now, through a friend, just been offered a Saturday job in a fishing tackle shop in Kettering, about 10 miles away. I was elated: a job! I could earn some money for fishing tackle, and it involved my passion, fishing. My Dad was keen for me to do this, and he offered to take me each Saturday. I loved it. I served on the till, although I was a bit shy at that bit, but my main job was maggots—gallons and gallons of them in a big walk-in fridge. Yes, most people's nightmare, but it really didn't bother me. I would riddle the old sawdust off them and add fresh to keep them clean, and the ones ready for sale would have maize meal added to **polish them off** and make them the perfect fish tempting bait for your hook. I liked doing this though; I would get them perfect out in the yard on my own. My other job was stacking the shelves. I loved this too: all that fishing tackle all nicely lined up, that was job satisfaction right there!

This went on for a while. Saturday mornings working, Sundays fishing, in between, day dreaming about fishing—my escape from the world. I read about government sports grants where young semi-pro sports people could get a grant to help them go professional. I got the details and applied. Back then, it was all done by reading books and magazines for knowledge and then writing and posting an application. I waited for weeks, in hope that this would enable my dream to come true as the end of school was getting close. I got the letter. Excitedly, I opened it. The reply wasn't at all what I expected. I was told that fishing was not considered a sport. I felt a huge sense of injustice!

I wrote a letter to the weekly fishing publication, the *Angler's Mail*, and they interviewed me and ran a quarter-page article on me, even interviewing an influential person from the world of darts. The headline read, **'SLING YOUR HOOK, Grant-plea youngster told fishing isn't a sport!'** It's now actually very much classed as a sport in the UK, with matches live on ITV 4 and Sky Sports, with prize money exceeding well over £100,000 for a five-hour fishing match!

The Police Arrest

Things were about to take a turn for the worse in the Simpson household. Mum and Dad were arguing much more. I knew it was all money related. Money was so tight that meals were basic, days out non-existent, as were holidays. My mum was suffering from what I now know as depression. I overheard her talking about being in a **'big black hole'**. I spent most of my days in my bedroom alone, apart from those days I could go fishing; they were the days I lived for.

One evening, my Mum and Sister were nowhere to be seen. They had disappeared. Dad and **I** were at home. We had just eaten, I can't remember what—probably beans on toast! Then suddenly, there was a knock at the door. It was the Police. My heart raced. I panicked. What had happened? Was it something to do with my Mum and Sister? There were two Police cars outside. One of the officers told my Dad he was under arrest for assaulting my Mum. We were both in shock. I started panicking and crying. I was only 16, a quiet, shy and timid lad that had never been in trouble, and I knew I had not seen anything go on. Dad was put in handcuffs, and I started screaming, **"No, no, don't take my Dad!"** My Dad looked shocked and confused as to what was going on and told me I'd be OK. Another Police Officer held me back. I was crying my eyes out, shaking and sniffling, not knowing what the hell was going on.

I was then told I was under arrest for assaulting my Sister. I was confused. Why was this happening? **This wasn't true.** I was put in the back of a Police Car, absolutely terrified of what was going on. The Police car started to drive out of town. I was hysterical. I asked where they were taking me. **"Weston Favell,"** they said. **"We can't take you to Wellingborough as that's where your Dad is going."**

"Stop crying son, you'll be OK," said the officer.

I was shaking. I felt sick. I was so incredibly scared. The electric gates opened, and we drove through to this large Police yard, in a town I had hardly been to. I was petrified. I was taken into the Police Station, and the handcuffs were removed. Still crying, I was booked in by the Sergeant and taken to a cell. It was horrific. There were men in cells next to me shouting, **"Sarg, Sarg, open the fucking door!"** and people were kicking and punching cell doors. The lights were bright, and the noise was horrendous. I sat there absolutely sobbing my heart out, rocking backwards and forwards. My whole world had just fallen apart. I just didn't know what was going on. This accusation had no truth whatsoever.

A few hours later, they took me to an interview room and asked me what had been happening. I told them that Mum and Dad had been rowing, and they asked me about him hitting her. I hadn't seen this at all, but they kept pushing. I kept telling them the same things whilst continually sobbing. Then they started to ask me about what I did to my Sister. The answer was **nothing**, that was the truth, absolutely nothing. I didn't know where all of this had come from. Next they asked me about food being locked away. I was confused. I had no clue what they were on about. The food was in the cupboard, fridge and freezer, where it always was—not that there was much of it at times. The interview went on for quite some time, but I just didn't understand what was going on. I was then taken back to the cell. Again, the noise and light was horrendous. I was in an absolute mess!

A little while later, I was collected by an officer who said he was taking me to my Nan's. I asked why I couldn't go home. I was told I wasn't allowed; my Mum didn't want me there. My whole world had just fallen apart! I arrived at my Nan's. She made me a sweet cup of tea and comforted me. I was just inconsolable. Around midnight Dad turned up. I never really hugged my Dad: we were never a huggy family, but I ran to my Dad, hugging him so **tightly** and crying my eyes out! I asked him what was going on. He was as baffled as me. From now on, we would be living at my Nan's house, Dad and myself sharing a double bed.

Days later, it transpired that my Mum had mentally broken down in the police station and told a lot of untruths. She had said that my Dad and her had a row and he pushed her and hit her, and that I had then pushed and hit my Sister. Mum had also said that Dad had been locking food away and not letting her eat! Of course, all charges were dropped; however, life would never be the same again. I wasn't to ever speak to my Mum for well over 3 years after this point, despite her constantly writing me letters trying to apologise. How could I talk to her? She had just ruined my life!

The Failed Tradesman

Dad and I lived with my Nan for a while. I secured my first job there; it was as a **trainee felt roofer**. On my first day, I walked across the park in front of my Nan's house, so nervous, ready to be picked up at the meeting point I had been given, my stomach full of butterflies and my mouth dry. I saw the van turn up and went to get in. **"There's only three seats up front, lad, you need to get in the back,"** I was told by this burly guy. I opened the door of the van and clambered across rolls of felt and tools, and sat upon one of the rolls of felt. We headed off. I was scared. These were big, tough guys; I was this chubby, weak, shy little boy.

We travelled for about an hour and got to a school. I was told to go up the ladder and start helping to scrape the old felt roof off. I had never been up a ladder before. I was scared stiff and shaking. I tried scraping but really struggled, so they did the scraping and got me to chuck the rubbish down into the skip. It was exhausting. My mouth and throat were so dry they were sticking together, and I had dust and grit in my mouth and my eyes. It was horrid, and I felt frightened. The guys were just grafting, laughing and singing along to the radio, making up different words. I remember Queen's 'Living On My Own' playing full blast and they were singing the part that went 'Dee do de, de, dee do de, de' as 'little ol lady, little ol lady".

Next, I was asked to carry rolls of felt and kegs of bitumen up the ladder. Again, I struggled. I just didn't have the strength or the physical ability to balance up that ladder.

I was so glad when the day was over. At times, I felt my bottom lip quivering. I was in a whole new world I was totally underprepared for. I got home. They dropped me off, and I just couldn't hold the tears back as I walked across the park. It was a horrible day. I tried to hold it back when I walked into Nan's house, but it all came flooding out. I ran upstairs to the bed. I just wanted to be on my own. The noise, the shouting, the physical exhaustion—it was just too much.

I got it together for the next day and took the trip across the park again. This time, sitting on the felt in the back, we took a different route, out to a village and this time to an old school with a big apex roof. No flat roof this time. This time I was asked to tap clout nails in at the top of the roof. I was shaking so much that I hit my hand a couple of times! Again, it was a horrendous experience, and the guys made no bones about making fun of me. I was their new entertainment. I was useless!

That evening, after trying to pluck the courage up for what seemed hours, I phoned the owner of the business. I asked my Nan if I could use the phone in her bedroom. I knew this was going to be painful. I pulled the piece of paper out of my pocket. I shakily started to dial in the number. It was one of those really old phones with a dial you pull around with your finger for each number. My stomach was doing somersaults!

"Hi," I said shakily, **"it's Gavin. I don't think the job is right for me so I don't want to come back."** He replied in an instant: **"Ah, that's OK. I was going to sack you anyway as the lads told me you were fucking useless. See ya!"** The phone slammed down! I was shocked for a moment. I just couldn't get my breath. I knew I was useless—my teachers told me I was useless, my Dad told me I was useless, my Mum and Sister didn't want to know me anymore. It was just a shock to hear it in such a way that it came across. I felt sick. What should I do next? I'm useless.

Chapter 4 - Into The Factories

I started to visit the job centre daily and read the local **Evening Newspaper** looking for work. I had to get a job. Dad and I were basically homeless, living at my Nan's. I had to start paying my way so we could get a place to live. I filled out application after application. Nothing. Not a single phone call or letter; email didn't exist.

My Dad looked at an application. He said I was being too honest and I'd never get a job like that. "But I can't lie, Dad," I said. "I don't have any qualifications; I never collected them. That boss did tell me I was useless too." "**NOOO**, you can't put stuff like that down, Gavin. You will never get a job," my Dad said, shaking his head. He said, "Look, no one actually checks your GCSE results. They don't mean anything for people like us. They are only if you are going to get a good job; just make it up." I really didn't want to lie. I hated it; I just really struggled with it. However, times were really hard and we needed money.

The Empty House

A few weeks went on and finally Dad said we were moving back home. Mum had moved away, back to Cambridgeshire somewhere. I was elated: back to my home! Okay, it wouldn't be quite the same, but I'd have my own bedroom and all my stuff back, as all I had was a black bin bag with some clothes in and my fishing kit. We walked in. I felt some excitement. Then, as I walked from the hallway into the lounge, it sounded different, bare, and there was a bit of an echo. I turned the corner to find a bare room. Nothing. Absolutely nothing. All of the furniture had gone, even the gas fire that was fitted in the house when it was new—gone, just blocked off pipes ticking out of the wall. It turns out Mum had sold everything, even the fire. My bedroom was bare; all my belongings and furniture had gone, the whole lot. I still had just a black bin bag full of clothes and my fishing kit, nothing else! I sat on the floor, my head in my hands, just feeling broken.

We went back to Nan's for a while; we couldn't live there with no furniture or heating. I continued to look for work and finally got a job in a local factory making **double-glazed windows**. I had the job of putting the rubber seal into the frames and sashes. It was great: I was earning money. We needed it more than ever now.

Buying a New Identity

I walked the four miles to work and back every day. The weight started to drop off of me, and I needed new clothes. I remember going to Burton's Menswear. I had never bought clothes before; Mum had always done that. I felt so panicky in the shop, embarrassed that I didn't know what to buy, what went with what. I didn't want to appear different; I wanted to blend in. I looked up and saw a mannequin dressed in black jeans and a green shirt. I spotted them on the rails, and there were two colour choices for the shirt. *That'll do, I think. They go together, right? Ahh, now, what size am I?* I had no clue, so I took some clothes and very nervously asked if I could use the changing room. I was so nervous; I felt really out of place. After a few attempts, I found some clothes that fitted me and bought them. I'd never been good at fashion and just didn't know what looked good or went together. I still didn't for many years, which you'll hear more about!

A month or so later, unfortunately, Nan's neighbour passed away. Her daughter had been around and seen us. She needed the house cleared as it was a council house, so they wanted to give it to someone else to live in ASAP. Dad offered to help her clear the house if we could have the furniture etc., instead of it being taken to the tip. She was delighted, and it helped us all. I remember clearing the house; it smelt of cigarettes!

Dad managed to get a van to borrow, and we cleared the house, taking anything we needed that the family didn't want. We had a three-piece suite, beds, a wooden wall unit—one of those with a built-in cocktail cabinet with a mirror at the back—and even some ornaments, like a shire horse and a cart and glass fish, proper 70s. It was starting to feel like a home again, just not quite our home!

The False Friendships

I carried on with my job in the factory. I gradually started to learn new areas, from steel reinforcement cutting to plastic welding and corner machining. However, this is where I started to make friends—or so I thought! The walk to work was giving me time to think, trying to work out how I could fit in. I felt like an alien. I just wanted to be like everyone else, to look the same, to dress the same, and even get a girlfriend. I was just so nervous though; just speaking to a girl was almost impossible. The huge anxiety would just take my breath away; I just couldn't speak. *Why couldn't I just be cool like the others?* I started smoking to be in the cool gang, and I'd share my cigarettes out; we'd go out drinking.

My Dad currently didn't have a car. His car had failed the MOT, and as I was earning some money and starting to take driving lessons, I decided to buy a car, let my Dad give me some additional lessons, and allow my Dad to use the car as if it was his. I paid £150 for a MK2 Escort 1.3L in beige, including the cement that was stuck to the carpet in the rear footwell!

I was still doing the odd bit of fishing in matches on the weekends, but my main thoughts had turned to how to be liked and how to get a girlfriend. It just wasn't easy; I felt different to everyone else.

The Professional Angler's World

I picked up a sponsor and joined a local team called Bedford Pro Rods. It was pretty exciting as it had some of the region's top fishermen in the team. I'd started to appear in local and national angling press as I started to win more matches, and my Mum had started writing to me and sending me paper cuttings she had seen of me when I had fished across in Cambridgeshire. It took many, many months before I was to ever reply to her; I was just too hurt from what she had done.

I had got invited to the opening of a new fishery called Castle Ashby Fisheries, by the owner, Mick. It was a three-day event consisting of over 200 anglers, and each day you would fish a different lake out of the three there. I was honoured to be invited as there were some real top-flight professionals there, including an International angler from Finland called Jan Porter. He was really famous and in all of the angling press and had released videos. Also there was Ian Heaps. Ian became World Champion in 1975 in Poland, had fished for England for many years, had countless videos out and several large sponsors.

He also did roadshows all over the country offering tuition and offering a sales opportunity for Angler's World Holidays and his two main sponsors Sensas, a bait manufacturer, and Silstar, a fishing tackle manufacturer. Ian also ran occasional residential week-long angling courses. I had attended one several months before and had come home every night to get it cheaper as Ian lived fairly locally.

During this weekend, my Dad spoke to Ian about my desire to become a full-time angler and how it's all I ever thought of. Dad would speak for me a lot; I wasn't very good as I'd get too nervous. I'd even get verbally abused for that. One evening at a team meeting with my previous fishing team, Dad was talking for me and advocating why I should make the main team for the upcoming National Championships. One of the team, in his early twenties, pointed me out and said, **"Why don't you talk for yourself, you fucking muppet?"** I wanted to respond but the words just wouldn't come out; it was even worse if there was conflict.

Dad called me over. Ian had said he was looking for someone to travel the country with him doing his roadshows, setting up the displays, loading and unloading the van. This was it: this was my chance! I could get out of the factory and do what I loved. Ian said I could also take my fishing kit; we'd do some fishing on our travels, and I could also help him at his residential angling school he held occasionally. I couldn't turn this down! I said yes. We swapped home telephone numbers—there weren't really mobile phones or emails back then in the general population.

Dad helped me organise everything, all except handing my notice in at work. This gave me huge anxiety and knots in my stomach. This was one of the sorts of conversations I dreaded. I finally did it, and before I knew it, I was there, staying over at Ian's house with his family—wife Margaret, son Scott, and daughter Beth. I was really made to feel at home.

The Roadshows and the Checklist

We headed off, Ian driving as I still hadn't passed my test. This was an adventure, heading way up to Manchester. I hadn't left my home county of Northamptonshire apart from the odd family holiday. I remember the first time unloading the van well. I popped the van keys in the boot of the van in between unloading and shut the back door. I just wanted the ground to swallow me up. I was shaking nervously. What was I going to do? I felt like I just wanted to cry, but I knew I couldn't. I was in an unknown area, full of people I didn't know; I felt lost. I knew I had to just go and tell Ian. He wasn't too impressed, but someone managed to get a piece of wire, pull the latch up and open the door, and I had to then climb through to the back and fetch the keys. They had a really good laugh and made a bit of fun of me, but hey, what was I to expect? I just nervously laughed along, but inside I was breaking. I felt lost and in at the deep end, struggling to paddle.

We finally got set up and the show went well. We packed down and got to the bed and breakfast late. Ian liked a drink, so we often went to the bar or had a drink somewhere after grabbing some food and smoked some cigarettes. Then it was off to bed, a shared room with twin beds as it was cheaper. Ian was covering all of my costs and paying me just a very small wage. I'm not sure I slept much that night. Here I was, hundreds of miles from home in a cheap B&B, sharing a room with a man I didn't really know much. I just lay there pretending to be asleep until I actually was.

We travelled on, up and down the country from Newcastle to Devon and everywhere in between. I saw so many sights I had never seen before, and I was living fishing 24/7. The more time I spent with Ian, the more I would talk, and my confidence was starting to build. I had to speak to loads of different people each evening too, selling bits of fishing tackle, groundbait, raffle tickets, etc. It was great and so much easier because it was my passion; I started to lift and feel part of something.

I never locked the keys in the van again, but I did leave my suitcase in Newark and had to call my Dad and ask him to bring it to the next show in Peterborough! Every time I made a mistake though, I added it to memory. It would become part of a routine, going through everything logically to ensure I wasn't repeating mistakes. This would serve me well for many years, and still does now, as I run through a mental checklist.

For three months we travelled the country from bed and breakfast to the venue, set up, pack down, off to the digs, and repeat. On the weekends I'd even stay with Ian and his family sometimes, and I joined Ian fishing when I could. I made some great friends, all way older than me, but I liked that; I always seemed to get on better with people older than me and had great respect for them. I also got to work with some of my fishing heroes: 4 times World Champion Bob Nudd, a real gentleman; Ex World Champion Dave Thomas; and expert Rod Builder and industry legend Terry Smith. Imagine it: one night we had a curry after we'd completed a show at the Tower Club in Blackpool—me, aged just 18, and three ex-world champions of the sport I obsessed about, and a bunch of industry legends! It was amazing! I was one of them. Yes, some of them sometimes made a bit of fun; they could see I wasn't your usual 18-year-old lad, and that occasionally got me down, but that was banter. I just liked being a part of something.

Ian coached me, and I was getting ever better at fishing. I remember one day, I stood by Ian's garden pond, alongside Dave Thomas. Yes, two Ex-World Champions! Ian said, "Grab that rod out the garage; show Dave that shotting pattern we have come up with." I demonstrated it to them both and caught one of his fish from his pond.

One weekend I was at home between shows and I bumped into an old school teacher. It was Mrs Cooper, remember her? The only teacher that 'got me'. I told Mrs Cooper that I had, in fact, become a full-time angler, I was working for an Ex-World Champion doing fishing roadshows and had become friendly with some of the best anglers in the world, and getting paid for it! Mrs Cooper was really happy, but also very surprised. I wouldn't see Mrs Cooper again for many years. When I did though, she remembered this conversation very well, and it had a huge impact on her that I was totally unaware of at the time. We will hear about Mrs Cooper again later.

Eventually, I passed my driving test, and I could drive the van. However, very shortly after that, it was time for the roadshows to finish and for me to say my goodbyes. It was sad; I'd had such an amazing time and came out of my shell a little.

Returning to the Factory

I went back to the double-glazing factory, and they gave me my job back there and then. I started back the next day! I got back with my friends; it was great. I'd give them lifts, we'd drive about in the evening and go on trips to the coast. The more I did for them, the more they liked me. I'd never really had many friends before, and they even helped me style my hair and go shopping with me to help choose what clothes I should wear. Finally, I was getting there; I was starting to become a little bit more like everyone else, although even this lot would make fun of me at times for something I'd say or the way I had dressed.

With the desire to be more and more like the others, I ended up going out to 4 am drinking on a fairly often basis. The more I hung out with these friends, the more I saw things I didn't really like, and I'd get pulled over in my car by the police much more often. I'd started to fall out with my Dad over who I was hanging about with, but these were my friends. I shared my cigarettes, bought them drinks, gave them lifts, but they helped me to blend in. They helped me feel like part of something. With their help, I was starting to build confidence in speaking to girls. I was dressing much more fashionably. I didn't feel alone any more.

The late nights started to get more and more. Sometimes we'd be out all night, and eventually I lost my job from going in late. I became unemployed. I couldn't even afford road tax or fuel for my car. But I had a girlfriend. I was in with the cool gang. I was popular. This was great. I had never had friends and laughs like I had now; I'd do anything for these people.

The Spiking Incident

Eventually, I got another job, after many interviews. This time, I was working in a plastic injection moulding company. I started off on the coat hanger machine. About four coat hangers would appear out of the injection moulding machine, and before the next lot appeared, I was to clip them apart to separate them, then take one at a time, grab a metal hook and press a pedal that would push the metal hook into the plastic part of the coat hanger and stack them in a crate. It was non-stop but boring as hell!

At least I was earning again, and I could get out more! One night I was in a friend's flat in a not-so-desirable part of town. We were drinking and smoking and playing video games. They had a PlayStation 1 and we were playing *British Touring Cars*. Suddenly, everything felt very strange. It looked like the curtains were moving and flowers were growing out of them. Then they were all laughing at me as I kept crashing my car into the wall on the game. I didn't know why they were laughing though, as I was seeing a perfect drive around the circuit. I started to feel stranger and stranger and started to panic. My heart was racing; I was sweating. I didn't have a clue what was happening to me, but they were rolling on the floor laughing. One of them saw me panicking and told me that they had thought it would be funny to give me a sausage roll spiked with LSD! I panicked even more. They tried calming me down, but I wasn't in a good place.

One of them talked me into going home. It was strange walking outside; the lights were trailing everywhere. It was the strangest feeling I had ever had, and one I'd never like to repeat. They got me into a car, but I tried to get out while they were driving. I just couldn't work out what was going on; it was extremely scary. Finally, they got me home, and I remember sitting there all night in the lounge. I was alone as my Dad very rarely came to the house at this point as he had a new girlfriend. However, I did have a dog called Arnie. Every time I felt like the world was going a little distorted, I'd call Arnie over, and it would melt away, and I'd feel back on planet earth. I did this constantly all night until it got light!

This absolutely knocked me, and I suffered more and more with anxiety over the coming months. Things went downhill. I lost my job again and split up with my first ever girlfriend. I was absolutely heartbroken and felt incredibly lonely again: no girlfriend, my so-called friends had spiked me with hallucinogenic drugs! I broke down. I just felt so low. My Dad seemed to hate me for what I had become. I had no one!!

You might ask why I have included these last few paragraphs, but it's important to know just how easy it is for a young person that's

Neurodivergent to be taken advantage of. I was certainly gullible and just so desperate to have people like me that I'd do anything. This could be your child or, if you are in education, one you teach, or as a Leader, a young person you manage. Look for the signs and understand why they might be doing this. It may be that they are doing it just through **absolute desperation of wanting to have friends and be liked.**

Chapter 5 - A New Start

Rebuilding (Move to Mum's and Wine Warehouse)

I had no one. I needed someone. With apprehension I called my Mum. She was delighted to have me back and invited me to stay with her. She only had a two-bedroom terraced cottage in the middle of the Cambridgeshire fens, and so I'd have to sleep on the sofa, but I was desperate. I loaded everything up, my fishing kit, the lot, and went and moved in with my Mum.

I just did nothing for a while, tried to get myself back together, and catch up with my Mum and try and build back the relationship. Eventually, I got a job in a local wine warehouse, order picking, going around the warehouse with a trolley and an order list. It was okay; it paid me some money to pay my Mum and kept my car running. It only lasted a few months though, as I was laid off; orders had declined. I had this feeling that I wanted to learn a trade, like an engineer or a mechanic, as I quite liked cars, and taking things apart and putting them back together really gave me a buzz. I loved to truly understand how everything worked.

Trainee Fitter: Rules and Structure

I started to drive the 12 miles into Peterborough once a week and go to the job centre. One day I saw a job that was just what I was looking for: a **Trainee Tyre and Exhaust Fitter**—this was about to be the very start of discovering just what I could achieve! I had the interview with a Regional Manager from a well-known national tyre and exhaust business that, at the time, had a TV advert with a little jingle and fitters dancing in their overalls, singing a distinct line that was also written on the back of their overalls. The interview was unlike anything else I had experienced before. It was so focused on discipline and how you must look after your appearance, be clean shaven (times were different then), and be on time. It was full of rules and structure. **I actually liked it!** It kind of felt regimental, there was an order about it.

I started the next week. It was really nerve-wracking: new people, overalls to wear, and learning a semi-skilled job, a job of importance.

If I got it wrong, it could cause an accident much worse than a metal hook falling off a coat hanger! I felt smart in my overalls. I was part of something again. The lads were okay, but they could see I was a little different and naive. I really wanted to get in with them. If someone said something funny, I would say the same thing. I wanted to be like them. They were a close group and socialised out of work. I just really wanted to be liked and be a part of something. One day I repeated something—it was just my way of trying to fit in as I still felt like an outsider. The reply I got was,**"Are you a fucking parrot?"**

The Banter Test

I learned well. I took in everything and started to pick things up quickly. I loved it. The banter was a bit much at times, but I still kind of liked it as it meant I was a part of something. The banter, however, then started to get more and more. One day the Manager, a **tough-sounding Mancunian**, told me to take a fire extinguisher he had given to me to **KFC** across the road. He also gave me an envelope and said that they had re-pressurised it and I was to take it back along with the bill. I tried to question him as I wasn't sure this was right, but he raised his voice and demanded I go.

I walked in a crowded KFC restaurant, fire extinguisher in one hand, envelope in another, dressed in blue overalls. I got some strange looks. My heart was racing. I queued up feeling really awkward, and when I reached the counter, placed the fire extinguisher on it. I told the young girl that I had brought back the fire extinguisher and that I had the bill for them. The girl told me she didn't think it was theirs and said she'd get the manager. The manager came over, and I repeated what I had said to the girl. The manager also said he didn't think it was theirs, so I told him I had the bill and handed him the envelope. He undid the envelope and slid out a piece of headed paper from the company I was working for. He laughed hysterically and held it up to me. It said, **'Give me your chicken and corn on the cob before I squirt you ha ha ha'**. I went red, my heart raced more. I grabbed the fire extinguisher and headed out of the restaurant and back across the main road. As I waited to cross the road, all of the staff of the garage were standing outside laughing, tears rolling down their faces, and bent over double. I just felt massively embarrassed and totally gullible.

It hurt, but I couldn't let them see it; I just cracked on. I must admit, I find it funny now, and this was to be just the start of the banter I would witness in the tyre and exhaust trade. Before leaving this place, it would get worse to include being cable tied to a chair and smeared with grease in places I won't mention and a cardboard box put on my head.

It was also here that I learnt a lesson that would become valuable many years later. It was the manic tidy up and cleaning that happened when a local branch called to say that the Regional Manager was doing his rounds. It was a manic rush to get everything perfect; even the tops of the doors in the office would be checked for dust. Many years later, I have been much more in tune than many about the reality of a business: what the bosses see and what happens are very often two very different things, depending on the manager you have in place.

A Better Mentor

A few months later my Mum, out of the blue, said I couldn't stay there any more and I had to be gone within three days, by order of her landlady. I'd finally found a job I loved, albeit for the banter. I spoke to the Regional Manager about getting a transfer, as the only place I had to live was back at my Dad's house, which was now mainly empty. He told me I should grow up and buy a flat in Peterborough. I just couldn't do this; I had to live at home, be that with my Mum or Dad, I just wasn't ready for this. For a few months, I drove 50 miles each way, every day. This included every other Sunday too—those were some very long days.

Finally, I got a transfer. I was now working just a few miles from home; I got some time back. The experience at this branch was totally different. The manager there, Tony, was not the sort that would encourage banter. We had a laugh when we weren't busy, but it was serious work and certainly no banter like I had received before. Tony was the first person in business that I looked up to and wanted to be like. He was so great with customers and so professional, such a kind guy and helpful. This is who I wanted to be. I got really good at my job quite quickly and then started to be sent away on courses to head office. I completed my **City & Guilds** in tyre fitting, exhaust fitting, brake fitting and suspension fitting over the coming years. I was even sent to other branches to help out and would be serving customers as well as fitting.

It was also here I was to meet the guy that is still my best mate today, Steve Cook. Steve would also end up being my best man when I got married—we'll get to some stories there later! Not long after I started at this branch, he left, but we stayed in contact and his friends became my friends too. A great bunch of guys, all a few years older than me. I went out with them occasionally. However, social anxiety was growing, especially as I started going out in town. I still wasn't the best dresser either. I was out one night and I was wearing a leather jacket I had **bought** from Matalan, the type with a fabric elasticated bottom. I know now you would tuck that elasticated bit under; I didn't then! They started to give me some banter, and I just didn't feel comfortable. I said I was going to the toilet and disappeared out of the back door. I just felt sad; I wanted to be liked. I walked home feeling down and emotional and spent the rest of the evening on my own. Next time they saw me, they had assumed I had gone off with a girl. Ha, not a chance of that! What girl would like me? However, I went along with it, and they were always of the belief that is what happened, unless of course they read this book!

The Magnum Tyres Family

Steve had moved to a local independent tyre company called **Magnum Tyres**. I can name this one as it no longer exists. Magnum Tyres was the best place I have ever worked. I made friends for life there and met the next person I would look up to in business, Glenn Pack. We are all still in regular contact nearly 30 years later and meet now and then for a meal and a few drinks and have an active WhatsApp group where we still laugh about the things we did. There were two Steves, one known as Wib and my friend Steve known as Bunter, Glenn, often known as Dooby, and Jaffa, who if I told you his real name was Alan, he would hate it—oops, already did, sorry Jaff!! In fact, it was here that Steve had picked up the name of Bunter. Bunter, Dooby and Jaffa even had their names signwritten on the side of their company vans. Later to join us would be our apprentice Mark, known as Little Mark, and also Mick, known as Little Mick. I have never worked with a bunch of guys that were like family as this lot are and doubt I ever will again. It just didn't seem like work. Yes, we would get it done, but often we would be laughing so hard our stomach hurt and tears were rolling down our faces. We even all went out at weekends together as a group. At first, I struggled with the banter; it was pretty full on, but it was Bunter that helped me reframe it. He told me that they were doing it because they liked me. If they didn't like me, they wouldn't feel comfortable having such a laugh. I'm not saying I reframed it instantly, and I did struggle with it at times, but eventually I got it and would even become an instigator at times!

Magnum Tyres was more about **truck and plant equipment tyres**. We would fit tyres on everything from vans to combine harvesters, earthmovers and everything in between. Even the customers here were like friends and would even be in on some of the banter, and even the ones receiving it. The banter was different here. It wasn't just one person that got it, we all did, although I got a fair share. Some of the stuff that happened I just couldn't repeat here; however, I do have some stories to share that might make you laugh.

The Ultimate Prank

One morning I was the first one there. I had keys as I used to be on the rota for night-time breakdowns. I unlocked and started to get the place ready for business that day. As I **did** so, the office phone rang. It was Glenn phoning in sick—that was highly unusual. I wished him well and cracked on, thinking, *right, I need to step up today*. Next, Bunter called in sick. He said he had been with Glenn over the weekend and must have caught something. He sounded really groggy. I carried on getting set up, opening the roller shutters and starting business. The first customer turned up wanting a new tyre, and then at the same time, one of the regular customers, a haulage owner, called. He had a truck with a puncture on the side of the road and needed someone there fast as it was in a hazardous position. I told him the situation, and he said he couldn't help that and he wanted someone there now. He was known as a real hardman and said it how it was! I told him I would get something sorted and call him back. The phone rang again; it was Jaff calling in sick. I said, "This is unbelievable! I have Brian on the phone going mad, he needs someone out right now, I have two customers waiting outside now." The panic was really setting in.

I put the phone down, went to serve the customers outside, and the whole bloody lot of them appeared round the corner holding their bellies, tears running down their faces—it was a wind up! They had all been sitting in the canteen behind our industrial unit; even the customers were in on the joke. I was a little stressed out, but, looking back, it was hilarious. It was all done in good humour. Despite being the butt of a lot of jokes, I could tell these guys meant no harm. It built a huge bond that we still have today and they still give me banter, but I give as much back now!

There were so many other things that happened that I could probably write a book about it, and the things we did still come up in conversations today and still give us belly laughs! I'll share with you another example. We would use, as part of the job, an aerosol brake and clutch cleaner. It was flammable but burnt out really quickly. There was the odd occasion where someone would spray a small squirt on the back of your fire-proof overalls and light it. It would go out within seconds. Yes, very dangerous, and I'd never condone that behaviour now, but we all found it highly amusing. One day I was on the phone to a regular customer and Bunter, usually the instigator, sprayed some on my back and lit it! I put the customer on hold to put myself out and call him a few names and carried on the call, so professionally! Many years later, Bunter is now a health and safety representative for a large utilities company. Yes, we were all in disbelief too! Anyway, he is good at his job. However, on the way up the career ladder at work to where he is now, he was on a health and safety training course. They were talking about banter and how it can get out of hand and asked for any examples. Bunter explained that he once set a work mate alight while he was on the phone. The host of the meeting asked him to mention something that had really happened. He said, **"It did really happen, I set my mate Gav alight!"** However, you will be pleased to know we have all grown up, a little, and would now never condone that in a place of work, or in fact anywhere!

The Workplace Reality

To many of you that haven't worked in a garage or on the shopfloor, it might sound outrageous. However, many things like this still go on, and the experience and knowledge of this has really helped in business as I've grown. I get the culture, I get the people, mostly, and many colleagues that haven't lived this life would just never get it, and many don't see it as if any office or senior management come into a building, you never see the true workplace, I can assure you of that. The amount of times I have worked in national businesses at that level and branches phone each other to tell them if a Director or Regional Manager is in the area. Suddenly, it's all hands on deck; you never see the true picture.

I worked at Magnum Tyres for a number of years until finally it was sold out by the owner to a growing chain, the owner of which was building a business through acquisition with a plan to eventually float the business on the stock exchange. Suddenly, overnight, it changed. A new manager was brought in. No more laughs. The hours were long, and you were managed, harshly. There was no more feeling of a family that got the work done and would do anything for anyone. Even the customers saw the difference, and many left. I remember being forced to work on Sundays for the first time. The hours were long as they had lots of large fleets they looked after, and even if you had been to several call outs through the night, you were expected to crack on as normal. The conditions got worse until everyone left. All of us went our separate ways. Jaffa had started his own business, which is still successful today and took many of our old customers with him. Glenn, Bunter, Mick and Mark went to work for a national business doing the same work with Glenn as the manager, and Wib went to work for a local truck suspension business that was one of our customers. The business that had brought Magnum out continued to grow for a while, but the company didn't get on the stock exchange and is now dissolved. The difference was, despite the messing about, we cared. Our customers knew it. We treated each other as friends and still do. No micro management, no politics. We had fun, but we turned a profit!

Meeting Kerry: My Rock

During this time of my life, and while still at Magnum tyres, I would meet someone that would change my life, and she still does every single day. Without her, I am pretty sure I wouldn't be here! One day I was a little bored at home. I spent a lot of time at home. A friend popped around and invited me to come and play pool that evening with some girls he knew. He picked me up later that evening, my belly full of butterflies, and we met Kerry and her two cousins.

That was 27 years ago. We are now happily married with three children. Kerry is my absolute rock and was a huge turning point in my life. Kerry started to bring me confidence. She had my back from day one. She was and still is my fashion designer—I'm still rubbish with clothes—my best friend, my confidant, my lover, my absolute everything, I absolutely adore this woman. This is why I dedicate this book to her. Without Kerry in my life, I would never have achieved what I have. In fact, what **WE** have. Kerry was to change my life! Kerry, I love you! I'll end this chapter here, but you will hear much, much more about her as we move on.

Chapter 6 - The Pivot Point

The Reality of Masking

With Kerry building my confidence, I was starting to change and realise I had more in me. Kerry also helped me start to deal with my social anxiety. Yes, despite good friends, I would still get this in pubs and clubs, and more importantly, I was obsessed with what people thought of me; I just wanted to be liked. I remember so many parties and wedding receptions I just couldn't go to. I was quite anxious at times. For example, if something was wrong in a restaurant, I would never complain. If I couldn't find anything in a shop, I wouldn't ask. You might ask, *how did you work in the rough and tumble world of truck tyre fitting and deal with all that banter?* Well, I was two different people. When I put on my overalls, I was Gav the tyre fitter; with them off, unless with my trusted friends from Magnum Tyres, I was a very different person. No one knew this though, except for Kerry; she saw the real me. Many, many years later, I understood this to be **masking**—trying to fit in and blend into an environment. For so many years I tried to be the person I thought people would want me to be and, like most in any situation, I was a different person in different groups of friends. They could never meet as I had different personalities. It was hard work, exhausting, and consumed my every thought.

I was never really happy with who I was. I'd be down a lot and want to just be at home and not go out. This could often be a challenge in a relationship, but Kerry got it and stood by me; we would have many cosy nights in. When I did go out, I had to drink. I would drink before I went out to calm my nerves and drink a lot, just to enable me to be there. I never became dependent and I didn't drink at home on my own, but I was certainly a binge drinker and for the wrong reasons. During this time, I learnt what depression was, and anxiety. This was through a leaflet I had found by a local youth organisation called Service Six. I had never heard of these terms before, but these leaflets explained just how I'd felt. However, I didn't tell anyone, apart from Kerry; I was embarrassed. There was a lot of stigma about mental health then. Several times I would book a Doctor's appointment and try to tell them; I just couldn't, despite needing help. I had to just crack on and pretend. One day, I finally got the courage to talk to a Doctor. They told me to take vitamins, get lots of sleep, and try deep breathing. That was it; I felt deflated. They just didn't get it, and for many years I would just carry on struggling.

The Suit and the Social Leap

With the new company taking over Magnum Tyres and all of my friends disappearing, I decided I wanted to do something new. This was the point that I had decided I wanted something better for myself. I wanted to be more business-like. I had read a book by Richard Branson and was really inspired. It would be years later that I would learn of his Dyslexia and my own Neurodivergent diagnosis.

I knew I liked sales. My Aunty Beryl, who lived in London, was in sales for a business that supplied consumables to dentists. My aunty and uncle had a lovely house, went on fantastic holidays—I really wanted a life like theirs. I was also very good at sales. In one of the national chains I worked for in the tyre trade, we did lots of training on it. It was great as I had a script; I would follow it perfectly, and I would turn nearly every phone call into a visit to the branch. I was also very good at using my training and scripts to upsell when the customer arrived by ensuring I had fully checked their car all over and finding out their needs to sell them a better brand tyre should their use of the vehicle demand it. I looked for some local sales jobs, and one attracted me: it was a job as an **Estate Agent**. I thought it would be great. Kerry and **I**, now a good few years later, had **bought** our first home together and were doing it up. I had therefore recently been through the experience of dealing with an Estate Agent. I also loved the thought of wearing a suit for work instead of overalls and not going home at the end of the day with oil-stained hands. I went for the interview with my clammy palms, belly doing somersaults, and to my absolute surprise, I got the job. I was so excited; Kerry was so excited. I handed my notice in, and the very next week, that was it: I would start life as an Estate Agent. I really felt like I was going up in the world.

It was great. I got on with the team well. It was very different, very quiet, but I liked it; in fact, I loved it. I could sit there at my desk, absorbing every bit of information on the houses we had for sale so I could match the client to the home. I went on a great training course and was taught how to sell mortgage appointments, and also my all-important scripts and signs of a sale. Wearing a suit was ace. When I put that suit on, I became someone else, not just in my head, but in reality. I could walk in the same shop I had been in wearing overalls and be treated like a different person. Instead of the "yes mate," it was, **"Morning, sir, how can I help you?"** People spoke to me like I was worthy of speaking to; they assumed intelligence, whereas when I was wearing overalls, they assumed a lack of intelligence. This was so beneficial for my mental health. My whole life I had thought I wasn't good enough. My whole life I saw myself as a lesser person, not worthy of what others had or the life they lived. Never underestimate the difference it can make to someone in how you communicate with them. Today I make a point of holding doors open for cleaners, saying good morning as they pass and talking to the binmen. Trust me, it will make a huge difference to them and, without them, you would start to realise just how important they actually are.

Back to the Tools

I was fairly successful, and I was selling houses and mortgage appointments. It was a real buzz. I felt great. I loved it, but with a really low wage and commission, it wasn't very lucrative. Back then, houses were not expensive. In fact, we had recently bought our first two-bed semi-detached ex-council house for £38,000—that would hardly even buy you a garage now in the same area! I lasted about six months, but with having our first home, it was a struggle. Kerry was a car valeter for a fleet business, and our joint income wasn't great. I decided I needed to go back to what I knew; I could earn more money. I tried to hand my notice in, and they offered me some more money, but it wasn't enough. I knew I could earn more. I decided I wanted to be like Glenn and Tony; I wanted to become a Manager of a Tyre and Exhaust Centre.

First I had to get back into the trade. I called Jaffa. Jaffa wasn't looking for staff, but he knew someone who was, in a town about 15 miles away. Jaffa called the owner and called me back to say I had an interview. He then called back a few hours later to say: **"Don't worry about the interview, they will start you straight away."** I started the next week in deep winter. The van I had was an old Post Office 'Sherpa' van with a draughty sliding door on the side, no power steering, and the facilities weren't great either in the depot, certainly nowhere to keep warm and nowhere clean to eat lunch.

The work was heavy and dirty, and I didn't really like the boss. He was a hard guy and told you how it was. I didn't find it a friendly place to work. I often wondered what I had done! My mental health started to suffer. I had massive dark spells of depression. I was back in overalls and being treated like dirt on someone's shoe again. I often felt not worthy and strived to be that man in the suit again, but I couldn't. I couldn't afford it; I needed a decent wage. I had to pay my mortgage. This was it; I was back on the tools. This would be my miserable life forever.

The Breaking Point

One day I had to lift an earthmover tyre on my own on a site—you were expected to just crack on. My hands were blue with cold, my cheeks stinging with the ice-cold, biting rain, and I was standing in deep, sticky mud. I went to lift the tyre and wheel and my back went. It hurt. In fact, it hurt so much I wanted to cry and felt instantly sick; I have never experienced pain like it. I had to finish the job. I knew if I called to say I couldn't do it, I would be told to just get on with it. It hurt a lot. My back went into the most horrible spasm and locked up solid all on one side. I could hardly walk; I was bent over double. The pain was eye-watering trying to drive the van back to the yard, no power steering. The van was freezing cold, and the wind leaking through the side door—this was hell!

Back at the yard there was no sympathy, just a **"man up and get on with it."** I was off for a week or so after that. I never got any pay, and it was a struggle. It was dark and miserable sitting at home feeling like an absolute failure. I wasn't even capable of being the muck on someone's shoe right now. Often just sitting there staring at a wall, wondering why I carry on, *it's just not worth it!*

Thanks to Kerry never giving up on me and being there to try and build me up, I got myself up and out. She cared so much for me and would always be there—the light in my darkness. I went out and **bought** myself a weight lifting belt and did it up tight around my waist and just tried to carry on. I was on yard duties, which involved lifting tyres about. I struggled so much; I was walking bent over. The owner's wife, who ran the office, called me over and gave me a training leaflet on safe lifting and told me to sign it. I had to do it there and then. I carried on for a few weeks, just resting every evening, but it was terrible for weeks.

One day I was called into the office and was told, **"You fitted a truck tyre the other day for one of the Turkish drivers and the wheel fell off. Get your stuff, you're sacked."** I was in shock. I always torqued the wheels up and knew the importance of it. I tried to defend myself, but was cut short and told to leave the premises. I was in such shock. *What will I do? How will I pay my mortgage? I have a wrecked back too. What should I do?*

Reunion and Leadership Lessons

I called Glenn. He was still a Manager at the branch of a chain of tyre and exhaust centres, along with Bunter, Little Mark, and Little Mick, and some others I hadn't met. Glenn gave me the job. I could start the next day. There would be no interview! I was so happy; I had a job, but not just any job: I was back with my friends!

I started the very next day. My main job was to do the lighter jobs in the depot: car tyres, **exhausts, and brakes**, etc., although I would occasionally go out and fit truck tyres too. The conditions were so much better though. The vans had tail lifts to lift the heavy tyres in place, and health and safety actually existed! It was so great to be back with some of the old crew, and we got on from day one.

Eventually, I started to step up and have a more supervisory role. I wanted to help boost sales in the depot as it was very quiet and was mainly known for the truck tyres. This was my first step **in** managing anyone, and it didn't go very well! I had my plans to make this a great place for customers. In my head, I wanted to create what I saw Tony had created. I wanted to build the business for Glenn while he concentrated on the truck tyres. I wanted everything right. Unfortunately, others didn't share the same views. For example, some of the lads would 'read' (let's say, not suitable material) in the office or smoke in the office. I wanted none of that. I wanted to help create a place customers would want to come and feel welcome. Unfortunately, I had **failed to take** the others on that journey! Also, I hadn't grasped that when I asked someone to do a job, I couldn't just straight out say, **"Can you fit two tyres on the front of that Mondeo, please?"** The lads that I didn't know there weren't interested in what I wanted them to do; they just wanted to do what they wanted to do. It made me so stressed out. All I could think was that they were here to do a job, and if I asked them to do a job, they should do it. Back then I had no idea of trust or rapport or being a leader.

It was then that the Assistant Manager gave me some great advice and taught me how I need to first build that trust and rapport with the lads. Yes, they were there to do a job, but the way you asked had to be right, and you had to work on building a relationship with them. I took it in, but for a while I just didn't get it and found it quite frustrating.

Occasionally it would end up with a row and they just totally refused to do what I had asked. I just didn't grasp it. One day it resulted in Glenn calling John (obviously known as Little John) into the office one day and losing it with us. Now this made me stand back as Glenn was so laid-back and softly spoken. I worked to build a friendship with John and the others. The Assistant Manager was good with this. We had nights out etc., and Christmas parties. For one of them, we went to a casino night at a local football **stadium's** hospitality area. We did it in style though; we hired a limousine and all went in Tuxedos. Ben took a water pistol in a holster; he was James Bond for the night! It was a fantastic night, and we had many more fantastic nights too, and so the rapport started to build. In fact, I got on much better with John and built a good friendship with him. The team started to come together, just like the good old days at Magnum. It wasn't quite the same, but we certainly had our laughs. I started to relax a bit too, and my mental health improved immensely. I knew what I wanted to create, but I also knew it wasn't going to happen here. I needed my own Branch, and I needed to become just like Tony! I thought back to my Estate Agent days and remembered how great I had felt. I wanted to sell, I wanted to achieve, I wanted to be someone, I wanted to prove I could be more!

Chapter 7 - Management

I had such a strong vision of what the perfect Tyre and Exhaust Centre should be like, and I wanted to feel like a someone again and not a nobody, **so I started to look for management jobs.** I went over all I had learnt from my days with Tony and the way Glenn conducted himself. I had some fire in my belly, and I wanted more. I found a job working for another National chain of Tyre and Exhaust Centres. This one was purely cars only. Fully prepared, I put on my Estate Agent suit and headed off for an interview with the Regional Manager.

The Vision is Realized

He was impressed. I went through role plays of how I turn calls into customers, how I up-sell, how I control the stock, and how I deal with complaints. I was buzzing in the interview. I was explaining my vision of exactly how it should be. The Regional Manager was so impressed **that he offered me the job**. I was to have a branch in the town where I had worked before, where the racetrack was—in fact, just around the corner from the depot I worked at where I had hurt my back.

I was so excited for my first day. No overalls for me. Just like Tony, I would wear a shirt and tie. I put that tie on in the mirror with absolute pride and a beam on my face. This was it, this was my dream. No one was going to hold me back; I was going to show people just what I could do. I met the Regional Manager and he introduced me to the team. We did a full stock take, and I signed over for responsibility. This was it: I was a Manager, and I was so proud! I could finally create my vision!

What I hadn't realised, or in fact asked about, was the performance of the branch. It had been loss-making for a while and been through a few managers. The phone hardly rang, and opposite was a competitor chain that was constantly busy. The first day I had to deal with a customer complaint for shoddy workmanship. In fact, it was terrible. The place was a dump. The staff were clueless and just didn't seem to care. Some of them also looked very scruffy and unkempt—not the image I wanted us to portray, I wanted that professional look from the days working with Tony. No wonder it was making a loss! For the first week, I was so stressed I couldn't even eat my dinner when I got home. In fact, it was so bad on the very first day that I expected a TV crew to come around the corner and reveal it was all just a big wind up. It was ridiculously bad; I really wondered what I had done!

Towards the end of the first week, again I was dealing with customer complaints and trying my hardest to bring them back on side. The team just stood there, not a spark of energy in them. After one customer complained, I was so stressed out I kicked the bottom of the office door after they had left as I was so frustrated. I was just fuming. It was sheer incompetence that had caused it. The glass smashed in the door. I just wanted the ground to swallow me up. I had recently stopped smoking, so I asked for a cigarette and went for a walk to calm down and **collect my thoughts.** I just had to get out of there.

Branch of the Month

The following weeks were dark. I nearly gave up, but Kerry was there holding me up, telling me, **"You can do this," "Stay strong,"** and **"Keep going."** I really didn't want to be beaten. I had thoughts of how great I felt when things were right. This was my vision, my dream. I wanted to build the perfect Tyre and Exhaust Centre. I wanted to build my vision of perfection. I was proud of my manager's name badge, and I was going to keep it!

I started to plan my vision. I needed the staff to have some energy about them. I needed the place to be clean and tidy. I needed to ensure that every single job was done to the absolute highest standard. I put in controls. All wheel nuts were to be done up with a wheel brace and not an airgun so **bolts wouldn't be over-tightened.** All wheels would be torqued up to manufacturer requirements and then double checked by another member of the team. Exhausts would be double checked for rattles or blowing. Everything would be double checked. Not one customer would leave that place with a potential issue. One of the staff members looked like he had just slept the night in the park. I worked up the courage to ask him to wear clean clothes and get his long, tangled hair cut. He did it.

In between jobs, we would try and have some fun. I remembered I had to build rapport, but we would also work on improving the look of the building. We would also do training on how to answer the phone and how to turn a phone call into a branch visit, then when the customer turned up, how to upsell. I set the team targets, and soon it started to get busier!

We had hit another problem though. We had long wait times as we had two bays to pull cars into. One had a four-post ramp that would lift the car up, ideal for exhausts. The other, a two-post ramp that lifted the car up with the wheels hanging down, great for brakes, suspension, tyres, anything where you needed all four wheels off of the vehicle. The trouble was, if we got a job for suspension, we couldn't fit tyres and there was just a huge bottleneck that limited sales. Added to that, the tyre fitting machine was at the back of the building behind the tyre racks, as there wasn't space at the front due to the ramps. This meant you had to roll the wheels around the back, change the tyres, and roll them back; it was all too time-consuming.

We cracked though and started to get results. I started in April of 2003. We won the trophy for best branch in June. The regional manager, the team, and **I** were over the moon; we had completely turned this branch around! However, I wasn't happy to just settle there. I knew there was so much more potential. I needed to fix the bottleneck.

The Expansion

Just across the car park, just about a two-car lengths away and right in view of the office, was another building. It was basically a dump with roller shutter doors and was full of scrap tyres and exhausts, and basically just full of rubbish. I had a plan. I was going to turn this into two tyre fitting bays with a machine right there next to them. No more travelling, plus both ramps were freed up for more profitable work on brakes and suspension. I approached the Regional Manager with my plan. To my surprise, he was up for it. I had money for a skip to clear it out, a wall to be built to separate off the last bay for storage of scrap tyres and exhausts, a sign with our phone number on to put outside, and even a new tyre machine; we would now have two! This would, in effect, **double** our capacity. The team were quite excited and shocked at what we were achieving. You could start to see a buzz from them, even the way they held themselves changed, they started to have pride. I was beaming and in my element. For years I had wanted to achieve this. I knew what needed to be done; I just didn't have the opportunity.

We started work. If we weren't serving customers, we were working on this project. We had a builder in for the wall and painted that brilliant white. The floors were painted red. New tyre racking with our premium tyres right there in the bay, and two tyre fitting machines! Whilst doing this, we won Branch of the month again in July. Every day we were breaking records! Eventually the new bays were up and running and we won Branch of the Month again in August. The branch was now the most profitable it had ever been, and we had quadrupled the turnover! We were winning Argos vouchers, TVs, all sorts constantly through sales promotions. Every day we beat a record, I would take the whole team to the pub over the road and buy them a drink. I was in my element!

It was now starting to get really busy, and we needed more staff. I got an advert out, and the team asked around for anyone that would like to come and work with us. I interviewed several people in the little crew room at the back, sat on an old sofa—it's all we had! One guy appeared called Paul. His application form was terrible, almost illegible, and full of spelling mistakes. I interviewed him anyway, and we just got on. It turns out Paul was **Dyslexic**. I never knew much about dyslexia back then. All that mattered was he had good references, was absolutely mad about cars, I got on with him and so did the team. In fact, it was one of the team that told him about the job; they were really good friends.

Paul started working with us, and I immediately knew I had made a good choice. He was the most amazing problem solver and still is. Any issues we had, he would solve them; he was smart! He was also fanatical about Formula 1, and he and his girlfriend both worked as marshalls at Motor Racing events whenever they could, including the

British Grand Prix at Silverstone. We got on so well that we became friends. In fact, we are still the very best of friends to this day! His girlfriend Stacey is now his wife, and they have two fantastic children who are great friends with ours, and we still, over twenty years on, meet regularly at each other's houses and our kids have basically grown up together. There was just something with Paul, we gelled so well. The only other person I had got on with like this was Bunter. Later in this book, you will find, we all have something in common!

The Manager of the Year

One weekend Paul invited Kerry and **I** to Silverstone for the British Grand Prix. We had the opportunity to camp there all weekend as guests of their friends Johnny and Terry who were marshalling. If you have ever watched a documentary on Netflix called 'Schumacher' you'll have seen Terry. He's the guy with a bald head and a big beard holding up a blanket at the side of **Michael Schumacher's** car as the paramedics try to get him out after he crashed and broke his legs. Terry was hilarious at the camp site and had us in stitches. I was affectionately known as **'Paul's new Boss'** all weekend! It was such an amazing time, so much laughter all evening, mainly due to Terry! The noise of the F1 cars in the morning as they started to test them just sent the hairs up at the back of your neck. We were to marshall at Silverstone several times thanks to Paul, and I was even working on Parc Ferme for Lewis Hamilton's first ever British Grand Prix. I could have literally high-fived him as he drove past into Parc Ferme! In fact, one year Kerry's younger sister joined us, and it was there, in the camp site that she met her now husband!

Back at the branch things were going amazingly. The team had a buzz about them. We celebrated with cheers every time we beat our budget. We went to the pub right next door to our competitor and celebrated. We were winners, and nothing was stopping us. It just got better and better. This was it; my dream had been realised. I had proved that everything people had held me back from was right; my vision worked. I was later to discover though, that when you point a finger, there are always 3 pointing back and in those days of failure, much of it was down to me just not knowing the unwritten rules of relationship building. We won branch of the month again in September. In fact, we blitzed it. We were the best. The Directors of the business visited and congratulated us; they shook my hand. I was so immensely proud. At the end of that year, I was announced as **Manager Of The Year 2003** for the East Midlands Region and got the trophy to keep with a mini engraved shield for each month with my name on so many of them. It wasn't just me though; it was my dream, but the **team** delivered it, and I still feel immensely proud of them. The trophy sits proudly on a shelf above my desk where I sit here typing now, and it still makes me smile every time I look at it. I was on fire (not literally this time), **my team was on fire**, I loved life!

The Wedding Collapse

As our branch was doing so well, I was asked to go and run our **'Super Branch'**. It was a flagship branch in a much bigger town and was turning over £1m per year. I was delighted. At the same time, we were moving home. However, it all went wrong. Someone in the chain was abroad and uncontactable. It was a mess. All of our belongings were in a hire truck, and we had nowhere to sleep. We ended up parking the truck outside Kerry's Mum's house and sleeping in her caravan. However, I had to carry on. Work was my life and came before everything. I went there so eager. I was going to do the same here as I did in the previous branch. Over the coming weeks, I was on the phone getting people in. The staff were looking to upsell. The work was of good quality as I had put in the quality control procedures as before. Okay, not all staff were happy, and some left. They went with the previous manager to a competitor, but this allowed me to bring in my own team. I got Little Mark into the business as my Assistant Manager, a step up for him, and as I write this, he is still at the local branch of that same business as a Manager and has been there for over 20 years!

It was going really well. We were beating the budgets. It was so busy though. I would sometimes have three phones on hold whilst answering another and typing out a customer's bill. I could **NEVER** let a phone ring more than four times—to me, that was a failure. Every phone call was a potential customer. I did have one embarrassing moment though. I was so hyper-focused on multitasking, answering the phones whilst serving a customer, acknowledging others that came through the door, and I repeated back to a customer what he had said to check I had entered it correctly. I hadn't; I was trying to do too much. Correcting it, without thinking, I said, **"Sorry, blonde moment there."** It was just a phrase I'd heard and repeated parrot fashion with no real thought. The customer was blonde! He said, **"Err, what are you saying?"** Luckily with a smile on his face. Thank god he wasn't offended. I really started to think more about what I was saying at that point.

August 2004, and Kerry and **I** were about to get married. We had a fantastic wedding, although Kerry organised it all as I was just so busy at work, I regret that now; I basically just turned up. I was so proud and wanted to bring our families together. It didn't quite turn out like the **happy-ever-after** story though. My Mum and Sister came to the wedding but wouldn't come to the reception as my Mum didn't get on with my Aunty. I wasn't happy with this and decided my now Step Mum would be witness at the wedding and would sit at the top table. It was supposed to be the happiest day of our lives, and I was devastated that my Mum didn't want to be a part of it. On the day, one of my uncles had a go at me about it right before we were going to go in—not the tension I wanted on this big day and marrying the woman who had changed my life. We got married, Bunter as my best man. I was so nervous, Bunter just as much so—such an emotional day! It all went well, apart from I didn't know I had to do a speech, another unwritten rule, so I nervously just thanked my beautiful wife, the bridesmaids, and everyone that came along. I'm gutted about this now, to be honest, but you cannot change the past.

Bunter did his speech and spoke of the time at Magnum Tyres when I used to hide my lunchbox so he wouldn't steal my sandwiches. One day he found them and thought it would be a great idea to add some red hot chilli peppers to them. I grabbed my lunch to go on a call out and dug into the sandwich on the way. My eyes started streaming and I had to pull over, I just knew who it was! I got my revenge though!

To be honest though, it got worse. It was a deeply emotional and full on day with so many people to talk to and I was so overwhelmed by it all. I went to the bar with Paul and a few of my old team from the previous branch I had worked at and they started buying us Tequilas. I did one, then another, and another. In fact, we finished off the bottle. I think I was just done talking, and I was just burnt out from the day, it was all too much. I turned around and walked back towards the dance floor. The full effect started. It must have been the whiskey before the church, the champagne in the limo, the wine at the top table, the pints of lager that mixed with the Tequila! That's it. As I walked past the buffet, my whole world went hazy, and I fell to the floor, apparently nearly taking out the buffet.

I remember vaguely being walked up and down the rugby pitch, well, dragged by my Dad and Bunter's sister. I couldn't walk. In fact, I couldn't talk. I have never been so drunk in my life, and hopefully never will be again. The next thing I remember was waking up next to Kerry in a hotel. My mouth so dry, the feeling of a sledgehammer beating on my head, a cold sweat on my forehead and feeling like I wanted to be sick. I looked down and saw the wedding ring and thought, *oh shit!* To my surprise, Kerry was okay with it. Okay, she wasn't over the moon—I had ruined our wedding night—and apparently it was Bunter and another friend that carried me to my room, got me undressed, and put me to bed. Bunter's sister helped Kerry get out of her wedding dress and ensured she was okay. I was so sorry. I couldn't believe what I had done. Kerry got it though, she always did, I really don't know how she has put up with me and one day I want to really make up for this. The next day we headed off to Mexico on our honeymoon. We had the most amazing time in Mexico and came back refreshed and raring to go.

Bunter did tell me afterwards though that he wanted to play yet another prank on me that night: he wanted to pay for Kerry to stay in another room, leave me in there, and leave his boxers on my pillow! The man is an absolute joker, totally mad, but I love him to bits! We all laugh about this now, but I still feel so sorry for Kerry.

The Burnout

I got straight back to work when we returned. It was immensely busy. Sometimes, if the phone wasn't ringing or a bill didn't need doing, I was out there fitting. I was one of the lads; I'd even clean the toilets, but that's what got me respect. One day I was under a car changing the oil and a Regional Director walked in. He asked me what I was doing. I said, **"Changing the oil and keeping a customer happy.**

I'm one of the team. My team is busy, and one is having a break to eat some lunch." He wasn't impressed and told me he didn't want to see me under cars. I just didn't get it though. My customers were my absolute priority; that was my absolute desire: to have every customer walk out of there delighted and come back again and tell their friends and family. I didn't care if it meant I had to change oil on a car in a shirt and tie.

The business started to change. We were told we had to cold call from the yellow pages. Not quite so much internet going on then, and Facebook was in its mere infancy. I wasn't happy with this. It took me off of the phone where I knew I was best placed; it took me away from my customers. I would not do it as I prioritised my staff and customers and would be under immense pressure from management for not providing leads from it.

I was working **seven-day** weeks quite often at the time in order to give staff holidays etc., and there was one afternoon we were quiet. I just needed a break. I was starting to feel drained, and those dark periods were coming back. I was desperate for a haircut, so I whipped out. I got a call on my mobile; it was my Regional Manager. I felt sick as I should have been at work, but I knew everything was under control and I trusted my team. He knew I wasn't in the office as when he called it would usually be me answering, within four rings. I could hardly talk, my stomach was in knots. I had done something immensely bad and broken the rules. He told me, **"Get your arse back to that branch right now and make sure this never happens again."** I was so burnt out and emotional I just wanted to cry. I just needed a break. It was so immense and full on I really wanted the world to stop so I could just step off and take a breather.

I went back to the branch and cracked on. Over the coming months, the push from management was immense; my mental health started to go downhill and sales were declining. I started to get these strange sensations. When doing our daily mini stock take, in the exhaust racks I would wince at sharp edges like they were digging into my eyes. Everything was loud. The lights were blindingly bright. I just wanted to escape. It was relentless. I didn't want to be there. My dream had turned to hell. I was becoming a nervous wreck, and I just wanted the world to stop, I so desperately needed a break. There was more and more pressure on the cold calling and more pressure due to the drop in sales, and one day I lost it on the phone to the Regional Manager. I just couldn't do this anymore. I was an emotional wreck.

The Great Escape

I went home that day and just cried. I couldn't cope. I was struggling to function. I couldn't go back. I couldn't do this any more. I contemplated just taking my life and escaping from this hell. My dream was shattered. I was tired, just so tired. Everything was dark.

Kerry was so concerned for me and made me go to the Doctor. I dreaded this. I didn't want to talk about it, and I knew from experience the Doctor just wouldn't really do anything. I went though, but I was in a daze. Everything felt fuzzy. It was like I wasn't really there, just living in a dream, a not so nice dream. I couldn't function. My vision was hazy. I couldn't even remember driving there. I was broken. I registered on the touch screen. It took me a while. I had immense brain fog. It took me some time to just think of my date of birth. I sat there waiting, my hands fidgeting, broken. I didn't want to be here any more. My name was called out. It startled me. The lights were bright. I just felt like I was on the inside looking out. It took me a while to be able to even get to the right room in the surgery.

I sat down with the Doctor, my hands shaking, my stomach churning, and he asked me what was wrong. That was it, I broke down. I was a sobbing mess. I told him I couldn't go on. He listened, and he was so sympathetic. He explained to me that I had just burnt myself out and that things will get better. I just needed some rest.

I went home broken but relieved. The Doctor had signed me off for two weeks and told me I must rest. I went home and went to bed. I must have stayed there for a week. I couldn't even call in sick. I couldn't pick the phone up. Kerry did that for me and kept them informed. I slept and slept and slept. I even remember Kerry bringing me something to eat in bed. Those days were dark. The exhaustion was real. I was a broken man.

With Kerry's amazing care, after a few weeks I started to feel a little better, but I still couldn't go back to work, and I got signed off again. I was starting to think that money would run out and that I couldn't go back to my job. I was a failure. I tried too hard. I thought I was good. I thought I could better myself, but I was wrong. I was useless. I was ashamed of myself. Those teachers were right. I would amount to nothing. **I am Gavin Simpson, a complete waste of space!**

I needed to desperately rethink how I was going to earn money, but I just couldn't face anyone. I needed less noise. I needed headspace. I needed to be on my own. Then I thought about all of the HGV learner trucks that would pass the window of the tyre and exhaust centre. I had dreamed of that freedom during the later stages of working there. What if I could get a HGV licence and drive a truck? I could sit there driving and not talk to anyone. I could do that, and the money would be good as there was a shortage of HGV drivers.

I was also inspired by my Granddad and Great-Granddad—they both worked for the same haulage company, Fishers Of Waltham Abbey. My great-grandad was on the horse and carts to start with, and he was the first employee to get a motorised vehicle. My Dad was also an HGV driver early in his working life. He had worked for Tesco around London, in their really early days when they had little shops, no supermarkets, and Mr Cohen would give the drivers damaged tins to take home. Jack Cohen was the founder of Tesco, and the name Tesco came about from his wife Tessa Cohen, with the first three letters of her first name and first two letters of her surname. That was it. I was going to follow the family tradition. Added to this, during my time at the Super Branch, my friend Paul had left his job at the other Branch and become an HGV driver. He was loving it and earning good money. I was going to be a HGV driver. Maybe this was what I was meant to do all along.

Chapter 8 - The Big Wheel Club

The Pivot Back to Manual Labor

I wrote my notice out for the Tyre Company. Kerry delivered it; I just couldn't go back and face them. The relief of not having to go back was immense, and my mind immediately started to clear. That vice-like grip on my head started to loosen. I researched local HGV training companies and chose the best one. I always had to research, and now the internet was really coming along. I could spend hours researching; it was great and so satisfying.

I started my training. It was hard as I had to share a truck with another learner. I felt down still and didn't really want to partake in small talk, but I had to. I had to do this or we just couldn't survive. In the evenings I was applying for jobs. I couldn't be off work any longer; we had a bigger mortgage to pay now.

Towards the end of the first week, I had a call whilst on our tachograph break. It was the manager of a national waste company. They had dustcarts, commercial ones that emptied the big steel wheelie bins, skip trucks, and bulk waste vehicles. I was invited in for an immediate interview. However, I was a little nervous. I hated telling lies, but I had marked my last job down as being a supervisor. How could I try and get a job as a truck driver when I was previously a manager? They would never have given me an interview, plus I would have had to tell them I was a failure. No one would want a failure.

The Manager was very firm; he reminded me of the manager that had sent me to KFC that time—a real tough guy I really wouldn't want to mess with. He was looking at my CV whilst talking to me and noted that I was very well paid for a supervisor. I think I mumbled, **"Yes, they are very good payers."** The interview wasn't really much, and at the end he said, **"When can you start?"** Ah, now, this was a problem. I hadn't passed my test! I stated that I am actually doing my training this week and I had my test the following week. To my surprise, he said, "Well, we are just starting a cardboard collecting round using a **7.5 tonne** tipper truck with a cage on the back. How about you start work with us next week? If you pass your test, we can then get you on the bigger trucks." I was delighted, my heart was pounding. I shook his hand and was beaming. This was it: the start of a new adventure. My Grandad would be so proud of me.

Unfortunately, I failed my test with some minor points. I had clipped a curb with the back wheel, moving out of the way for an ambulance, and hesitated at a roundabout. Inside I was immensely nervous, and these were huge trucks. High up, the visibility was so limited around you. I still started at the waste company though and arranged some refresher days and a new test date.

The Reality of the Dustcart

My first day was in September 2005, and to start with I was out with another driver on a skip truck. This was to be for the first week, just to settle me in, get to learn the ropes, the paperwork, and the rules and regulations. A week later, this was it, I was out on my own. It was so daunting, but I knew my Grandad would be looking down on me. I had to make him proud.

The work was tough, out in all weathers. It was dirty and smelly. Yes, it was just cardboard, but often soggy cardboard, and at some of the Caribbean shops you'd end up with chicken feet and fish heads left in the boxes—it was gross! I was back again to the days of overalls, a nothing, a nobody. In fact, people treated me even worse. I was just a dirty, stupid binman getting in their way, and they made no bones about it. People would honk their horns, be rude to you; it was horrid. The only good thing was, I was on my own. I could have some kind of peace, just listen to the radio driving between jobs and not have to put on an act or be somebody else.

I remember one day, I was outside a shop. It was cold and pouring with rain. Traffic was trying to get past. I had the flashing lights going in the misty rain. It was wet and miserable. There were these chicken feet and mouldy fruit and all sorts still amongst this pile of soggy cardboard. I hated it. I just wanted to give up, but then I thought, *I can't. I have to keep going. I have to pay the bills. I'm a failure at everything else. This is what I deserve. I've just got to man up and get on with it.*

At that moment, I looked up and the shop next door was a guitar shop. I had recently gotten into playing guitar thanks to my mate Paul. He taught me how to play 'Wonderwall' by Oasis, and we used to have a right laugh with him making up songs, like the one he named 'Cabbages, two for a pound'. It gave me some peace and helped relax my mind. Kerry had bought me a cheap acoustic guitar from Argos for my birthday. I had always wanted a guitar, but Mum and Dad never got me one when I was a kid and Mr Wales, my teacher at Primary School, had also told me I was a failure when it came to music, I had no rhythm. As I progressed, I wanted to get an electric guitar. I wanted a Gibson Les Paul as I was really starting to get into Gary Moore and especially his epic song 'Parisienne Walkways'. Gary played a very famous Les Paul guitar. I knew I couldn't afford a Gibson, but in this window I saw a ray of light. I saw a black Gibson copy by a Japanese company called Tokai—it was a thing of beauty. Suddenly, the day seemed slightly brighter. I took my mind off the stinking, wet and soggy cardboard and focused on the guitar. **I was going to buy THAT guitar, and it was soggy cardboard that was going to pay for it.**

My mindset changed. I wasn't here to do a job I hated; I was here to earn enough to buy a dream. I worked so hard. I went to another HGV test but failed again, but I just kept going. Yes, some days were dark, but I just became obsessed with my Guitar. I could now play along to some of the parts of Gary Moore songs. I was getting lessons and teaching myself music theory. Whenever I was down I picked up my guitar. My problems would melt away, and I could feel myself starting to smile. A warm glow would take over me. There was something amazing about it. This would become my new obsession and would consume my every thought.

The Bogroll Express

Things started to come together at last. Yes, the work was hard, dirty and often cold and wet, but it was looking up. Some people treated me terribly in the street, but my obsession with guitars consumed my every thought. Eventually I passed my HGV test and I went into that shop and bought that guitar, the guitar that was a ray of light on a miserable day when I wanted to give up. To celebrate passing my test, Kerry and I went for a meal with Paul and Stacey. Paul made a toast to me passing my test and welcomed me to **'The Big Wheel Club'**. I was part of something again!

I remember my first day out on my own in a proper truck. I was so proud. All I could think about was my Grandad looking down, being proud. I would have loved to have spoken to him about his driving days, but unfortunately he had left us many years ago, but I just suddenly had a great connection with him I had never had before. Life was great. I passed my **City and Guilds** in HGV driving and had learnt to drive every truck. Paul had now followed me into the waste trade as the money was fantastic. There were no nights out sleeping in the truck, and despite the early start, you were often home by 2pm. I'd often see him at the local landfill sites and have a chat.

It wasn't all roses though. In fact, far from it, and it certainly didn't smell of them, especially when I was driving the skip truck and on the sewage run. My job was to collect the first two outfall skips from the sewage works. The first one was grit, basically the grit you would see as road toppings as it was washed away into the gutters. However, it also contained sweetcorn, which we don't digest so well, and tomato seeds, yep, gross. You would even get tomato seeds growing in the skips, and the skips steamed! Sorry to those that have just been eating or may be eating soon, but it gets worse! The second outfall was the other types of solids—no, not so many 'number twos', although there were a few that hadn't decomposed by then, but this was sanitary towels, toilet paper, and condoms in the main. You could feel the heat from it, and it steamed. It was gross. The worst thing was you had to lean across it to put a net over it and strap it down so it didn't spill on the road; failure to do this was instant dismissal. It was gross, but it paid an extra bonus. I even named my truck **The Bogroll Express**! On the plus side, I could see my mate Bunter occasionally who worked there now.

The Stress and Sensory Overload Returns

One day I really struggled though. As I drove down the huge hole in the ground at the landfill site with tonnes and tonnes of waste beneath me, all compacted and masses of seagulls hovering around, I tilted the skip up to tip out the steaming load and out popped a snake about four foot long from the skip and landed on the back of my truck. I was petrified! There was no one to help me and I had to remove it. I had shivers going down my spine; I felt sick, I was horrified. I had to climb on the back of the truck, get a shovel under it, and flick it over the side. I still get shivers thinking about this today. It wasn't the only animal encounter either. One day, on the dustcart, I pulled a bin out and a squirrel ran literally up my leg; I felt its claws, and often rats would jump out of the hopper towards you when you emptied bins. I just had to try and switch off from it. I had no choice but to do this; I was a failure at everything else.

There were some other horrid moments too. I once had a 12-tonne container of waste food slip off the side of the truck in a Sainsbury's yard while I was pulling it on with the hook loader and had to get a crane out to recover it. Another time I was on the top of a landfill site that was almost full. It was at the top of a huge mound and really exposed. It was so windy and snowing. It was bitterly cold. I was driving a **Scania** roll on roll off truck with a hook loader, like at Sainsbury's that time. I drove down the long bumpy track full of potholes and slush, up to the top and what we call the face, where we would tip the load for it to be compacted. The snow was driving sideways and it was bitterly cold. I pulled up near the face and reversed back towards it, went to open the door at the back before finally reversing up to the face and tipping. As I got out the wind slammed the door shut, and being an old Scania, the inner door handle, which would lock the door if you pushed it in, would get loose and as the door slammed, it locked it, with the engine running. There I was, getting pelted with sideways snow stinging my face, and the truck had locked itself with the keys in the ignition and the engine running. I couldn't call this in. I had to get the truck moving, and besides, I was freezing. I had an idea. I borrowed a screwdriver from the compactor driver, climbed up at the back of the cab near the lifting gear with the compactor driver watching and making sure I was as safe as I could be, prised the back window out and climbed through the little window at the back of the cab. I was shaking, and not just with the cold. I knew I was in big trouble. I should have stopped the engine and taken the keys out. I tipped the load and drove back with no window and took the telling off.

In fact, I was quite often in trouble and getting in sticky situations. I used to get lots of stick from everyone. I always felt a bit different to the others; I couldn't work it out. Was it because I had been a manager? I just couldn't work it out, but I never really did feel I fitted in properly. One of the drivers was ex-forces and had served in Ireland. You could see it had affected him. He was an angry guy, a very angry guy, and his driving was really aggressive! He used to shout at people to get out of the way and all sorts. One day I was in a dustcart with him and he shouted at a young mum who walked across in front of us as we were waiting to get out of a customer's yard. I won't repeat what he shouted, but it was horrendous. I told him that was it, I was getting a taxi back to the yard and I refused to work with him. I just felt on edge all day with him, and it would make my stomach churn. A few months later he got sacked on the spot for failing a drugs test—he wasn't alone, we lost three drivers that day!

The Inner Game and Final Crisis

My mind was firmly fixed on my guitars, and I was now playing in a local covers band and getting paid! It was amazing, I finally was part of something again. We even recorded in the studio and released an album, and I appeared on a local radio station with our amazing vocalist Natalie to play a live acoustic set. It wasn't easy for me and nerves were a huge issue, but I wanted this so badly and I wanted to prove to Mr Wales and to myself that I could do this. Music became my only source of inner peace. This was when I read my first self-help book, ***The Inner Game Of Music***, and I learnt that the voice inside my head was something the majority of people had. I had never spoken about my strong inner voice as I was kind of embarrassed about it. I learnt that everyone has an inner voice and it is that inner voice that can, if you don't train it, often be your most negative critic. I totally got this; it was certainly mine!

I would get nothing but stick about my guitar playing, it was my obsession and I would constantly talk about it. The other drivers would always make fun of me, maybe as I spoke about it so much, I didn't have as much self awareness back then or know that us Autistic people have a habit of boring people to death talking about our obsessions. One day, they left a little triangular guitar in the drivers' room with a post-it note on it saying **'Gav's company guitar'**. They had found it in a bin. However, that last laugh was on me. I thought it was a little unusual and researched it, I loved a bit of research. It turned out it was a rare **Russian Balalaika** and not a guitar at all. I sold it on eBay and made a healthy sum!

Meanwhile, my mental health was getting worse again. I wasn't socialising any more apart from playing in the band. The public were horrid to me if I was having to block the road. Customers assumed I was stupid as I drove a dustcart, and I was forever in trouble. The brain fog started again, and I made more mistakes. I took time off as I just couldn't face work and even didn't want to go to band rehearsals. I even started to find I couldn't keep the rhythm. Mr Wales was right, I was useless. I was just trying to be someone I wasn't, yet again. I started to withdraw into myself. I struggled with relationships. Life was going down the drain again.

Finally, I had to go to the Doctor. Mental health was being spoken about more often, and, although nervy, I also had a little confidence having read that book that many people can have a negative inner monologue. I sat in the doctor's surgery one morning and someone I knew from another band came in. I was embarrassed and wanted to hide. He could see I was down as he said, **"What's up, mate? You come to get some happy pills?"** I could hardly talk and just mumbled some words, wanting a hole in the ground to open up and swallow me!

The Doctor prescribed me anti-depressants. I didn't really want to go on them as I had been told they were addictive before and also there was a huge stigma, but I couldn't carry on. I kept going through these immense dark periods and was constantly ending up failing and going down a dark hole. The brain fog would increase, and I'd avoid all social situations. It was now affecting mine and Kerry's relationship. I started on them. It was really tough at first and I was on a real roller coaster of emotions. Some days I struggled to function and would phone in sick. I was all over the place. Eventually, it settled down, and it was like the clouds had started to part.

Chapter 9 - Sunshine Appears, Until The Clouds

It was now **2009**. After several months, I was feeling much better, and I was starting to have some hope. I was starting to go out again and met a friend of Bunter's called Steve—yes, another Steve! This Steve was a Director for a national courier business. He was right at the top, but in the local working man's club he was just one of the lads. He wore a baseball cap, got steaming drunk with us, and ate kebabs. The only difference was he walked about with a big roll of cash in his pocket! We got up to all sorts and became good friends. He had recently bought a cheap motocross bike, and Bunter, Steve, and a few others would go and have some fun on it at the weekends. They invited me one day. I had never ridden a motorbike before. I had a go. I was shaky and slow and kind of petrified, but I loved it.

Steve updated his motocross bike and gave me his old one. They invited me to go 'green laning', but I said, to do that, I needed to ensure I stayed totally legal due to my job as a HGV driver. At the time, I had time and money. I was earning well, and it had been almost six years that Kerry and I had been married. We had tried for children but had given up as we were told that Kerry had a medical condition, meaning we would probably never have children, therefore I was happy to just crack on with life and have an adventure.

The Gift of Hyperfocus

This gave me an opportunity for another mini obsession. I booked my CBT (Compulsory Basic Training), sat my theory test, and booked a direct-access crash course and a practical test that would allow me to ride any bike with unlimited engine size. I loved it. Out on my own, helmet on, and the feeling of freedom and solitude—I was totally hooked. Within a few weeks, I turned up at Steve's house fully legal on a 600cc Suzuki road bike. He couldn't believe it. This was an absolute case of **hyperfocus**, just taking something and eating, sleeping, and drinking it until I had mastered it. I was later to learn, this was a gift.

I got to know Steve really well, and at this point, I was out drinking with him every Friday night. There was another bike related event too, Steve blew the engine up on his bike. I said to him, "As you have given me your old bike, if you buy the parts and get me a Haynes manual I'll rebuild it." He couldn't quite believe what he was hearing, I said "It's fine, I love taking things apart and fixing them." We got the bike in my garage, ordered the parts and a manual. Within a week or two, in my spare time I had completely rebuilt his engine. He couldn't believe it. "How do you know how to do that shit?" He said. Yes, that's how he spoke when he wasn't in Director mode. You always knew if he had someone from work in the car if you rang him, it was a different Steve. He was just in awe and the next Friday he was telling everyone in the club what I did and what a smart arse I was. To me it was nothing special, just read a book and follow the instructions.

As we got to know each other more, we had many conversations about his journey to becoming a Director. As I learnt more about him, I discovered he had grown up on Luton's notorious Marsh Farm Estate and had certainly had an, let's say, interesting start to life. We spoke about how I started that journey into management a little, but I just couldn't do it and just gave up and went to be on my own in a truck. Steve asked if I missed being a Manager and said that he saw something in me and would certainly take me on as a Manager if I wanted it. This was the very start of planting the seed for me to get back on that journey and try to achieve something again. We also spoke about his journey of, what I now know as **social mobility**. I asked him, "How did you manage to speak like them, how did you learn the words to use with all those highly educated people?" He said that he just learnt as he went along, "you just pick it up." he said. Speaking to Steve made me realise that I might just be able to do it, and my dreams of self-improvement and growth once again started to appear.

The Miracle

I was enjoying riding the bike at weekends and had promised Kerry that after six months of being on the road I would take her on the back of the bike as a pillion. Kerry loved the bike, a deep blue Suzuki SV600 with full fairings, but I wanted to be absolutely sure about my ability before having her on the back. Well, I never did get to take her on that bike, as just a few months into ownership something amazing, and to us a miracle, happened to us. Kerry was pregnant! We cried with tears of joy; it was the happiest day of our lives. We were told we would never be parents and were even considering adoption, but this was it: we were finally going to be a Mum and Dad! I treated Kerry as an absolute princess, I still do. I worshipped her anyway, but this was epic; she was carrying our baby. This was so amazing! We made our plans and as the months went on, we decorated the spare bedroom. By this time, we were in a much bigger house in a nice area of town and had even factored in school catchment areas as part of wanting to have a family. This was it, we were set, the home was set, we had everything. We had waited for so long and at one time believed it would never happen, but the due date was getting closer, and the excitement was building.

Oliver is Born

One Sunday morning in August 2010, Kerry awoke early. "I think this is it!" she said. "I think we are going to have a baby." Kerry was getting contractions, and we were about to meet our son. We had already got a name; he was to be called Oliver, and we couldn't wait to meet him. We calmly but excitedly grabbed the hospital bag and informed Kerry's Mum and my Dad, noting that we would be in touch once he was born and that we just wanted some time together with him to share this magical moment as we had waited for so long. We drove calmly, but nervously and excitedly, to the hospital—well maybe Kerry was more nervous and in pain than me! We got there safely, and Kerry walked to the maternity ward, stopping occasionally as the contractions came. Kerry got registered, and we went to the room where I comforted her, but mainly felt like an absolute spare part and really felt useless as she was having the contractions. All I could do was hold her hand and rub her back. I loved this woman so much right now. A few hours later, Oliver was born, a beautiful little boy with jet black hair, at just over **5lbs**—small, but amazing. Finally, we had a child. We were beaming and holding this precious little bundle of joy.

Kerry went to make herself comfortable and have a bath while I just gazed at our wonderful little son when suddenly Kerry's Mum and Step Dad walked through the door. We were a little taken aback as we were hoping to share some time together, but it was great to see them and proudly introduce them to their Grandson, Oliver. They stayed for a while and then Kerry got moved to the mother and baby ward.

The Chicken Pox Crisis

A nurse came to check Oliver and Kerry over a few times, and suddenly there were a few doctors and nurses appearing. They were talking together and appeared to be discussing something about Oliver. One of them came over and said, "We have noticed some little marks appearing on Oliver. Just as a precaution, we need to do some tests." We waited for a while and then the time came that visiting hours were over. I was really worried, but I had to go. I had to leave the two loves of my life and go home. I headed home, got something to eat, and Kerry called. I answered the phone quickly. Kerry was crying. **"They took him away,"** she said. **"He has a rash. They have taken him to the special care baby unit."** We both bawled our eyes out. What was happening? Our precious little Oliver. We had waited over six years for this moment, and it was all going wrong. What could be wrong? I lay on the bed after the call, crying inconsolably. I have never been so upset in my life. Panic started to set in that we might lose him. I laid there and did something I had never done before: **I prayed**. I just hoped that there was someone out there that would listen. Please don't take our baby away from us. Kerry and I stayed in touch throughout the night; we just couldn't sleep.

I was there at the hospital awaiting opening hours. By that time, Oliver was fully settled in special care in an incubator, so from this point on, we could be at the hospital 24 hours a day, and we did just that; we never left his side. He was in a clear plastic incubator with wires coming out of him, a red rash all over his body, and a pipe coming out of his nose. We were both an emotional mess, but we had to stay strong for Oliver. We were taught how to feed him with a syringe through the pipe in his nose as he wasn't taking any milk, and he was monitored constantly by the fantastic team of doctors and nurses. This went on for ten days, and still we knew nothing as to why he had this rash or what was wrong with him.

Then that afternoon, a nurse came in and informed us that Oliver had to be moved immediately to the other side of the hospital and into the children's ward. We were shocked: *Why?* **"There isn't much time, get your things, we'll all take Oliver together and explain on the way,"** said the nurse. We went down into the lift and through an underground tunnel into the main hospital. The nurse informed us that they had grown some cultures to understand what was going on with Oliver, and they were astounded that he had **Chicken Pox**. "How can he get Chicken Pox so soon after being born?" we said. The nurse explained that they had never seen this before, but they were trying to understand a bit more about it, but for now, Oliver had to be moved out of special care as there were premature babies in there that he would put at risk.

We got settled with Oliver in a private room, and they fitted a cannula to his tiny little foot to administer **IV antiviral medication**. The nurse said that he was the youngest ever patient in the Children's ward, but they had to do this because of the risk. A Doctor came to see us later on and explained that due to the timing of the rash, Oliver must have contracted Chicken Pox in the womb, and it must have passed through Kerry's immunity and infected Oliver. At this time, and all through the pregnancy, Kerry was working as an Assistant Manager at a budget supermarket. This must have been how it happened as Kerry was working on the tills towards the end of her pregnancy as she was unable to lift anything heavy, so was having close contact to hundreds of people per day. The Doctor asked if he could write a paper on it, anonymously, for the medical journal, as it was such a rare occurrence. We agreed. We stayed in the hospital, occasionally coming home for changes of clothes; we were even showering and eating at the hospital. I had to take annual leave at work after the first week in special care and used up all of my holidays. I only had a week's paternity pay, but I wasn't going to leave him; he was so precious to us. We were there for three weeks before we could finally take him home. We had to ensure he was drinking milk and that his Chicken Pox was disappearing and no longer contagious. Money was the last thing we would worry about right now.

The Blame

We got home, got settled, and back to work, and life began to get back to some kind of normality. Oliver was a quiet baby, he never really cried, he was so easy to care for, we absolutely cherished him. I missed him so badly back at work driving the truck and I was thinking about him and Kerry all day. I had also used my annual leave so couldn't take any time off to support them or spend time with them, I felt a lot of injustice about that.

A year went on and Oliver was coming along well. He was a little behind on some things, but we were told that all children take their own path and develop differently. I was now, as a parent, thinking differently about work. I thought back to those conversations with Steve. I desperately missed my days as a Manager and I wanted to make our son proud of me. I also hated coming home having handled waste and sewage and absolutely stinking. I would take my work clothes off at the door and they would go straight in the washing machine and I'd be straight in the shower. I was so anxious about passing any bugs on to Oliver. I started to think that I was now ready. I was also really fed up of being on my own by now, especially with nothing to keep my brain occupied whilst driving, apart from not crashing of course, but I had been a binman for around eight or nine years now. *Who'd want me?*

Early **2012** and life was about to change again. Kerry fell pregnant with our second, Joshua. The pregnancy was fine, and birth was fine—well, for me at least, maybe not so for Kerry—and we now had a growing little family. The desire to progress and better myself was ever increasing. I wanted to make my children proud and support them and give them everything I never had. Oliver had just had his **two-year check-up** and there were a few concerns: he wasn't developing socially as expected. I began to blame the Chicken Pox—that was it. There was a reason our son was behind. The Chicken Pox must have affected him, and when I spoke to people, I repeated this often, embarrassed that our precious child wasn't quite like the others when other parents compared what theirs were doing at that age. I kept this narrative and just felt angry: *Why? Why had this happened to us, after all of the years of waiting, why is life being so cruel to us?*

Chapter 10 - The Path Of Discovery

The Leap of Faith

A job had come up in the office as a Traffic Dispatcher, creating the routes, communicating with customers and completing the drivers paperwork and logging their hours from their tachograph cards. I was interested. I was desperate to try and make something of myself once again. However, the money wasn't good, and it meant taking a **£20,000-a-year pay drop**. The work I was doing was very well paid due to the nature of it, but I really wanted this opportunity. I worked it out with Kerry, and we could just about manage if I took the job. Yes, the money was terrible compared to what I had been earning, but this was such a great opportunity. I could gain some skills here that I could use to get out of the waste trade and maybe get back into a job where I could progress. I knew that if I just tried to get another job now in another business for anything other than a lorry driver, no one would be interested in me. I decided to cut back as many bills as possible and go for it. This was it: I could stay clean at work, work in an office, and be respected, not treated like a lesser person constantly like I was out on the road. I decided that the benefits to my mental health would far outweigh the financial struggle I might have, and it would lead to much better money one day.

I applied for the job and got it. I was happy, but also felt a little sick that I had just given up all of that income, but finally, after nearly 10 years of driving dustcarts and skip trucks, this was it. I was back wearing a shirt for work, it felt so damn good.

The Excel Hyperfocus

I started in August of 2013. It was great working in the office. I could eat lunch without the stench of waste or sewage. I could drink a nice cup of tea out of a porcelain mug, and I wouldn't get soaking wet or freezing cold during the winter. My boss asked me if I knew what Excel was as I would need to use it. I had no idea. I had a look, but just saw it as a grid you could type into, and it could do sums too, just like a calculator.

That week I was due to go on holiday. We were taking the kids to Disneyland in Paris—a final family treat before we really had to pull the spending in. En route, in St. Pancras Station, we went and got some snacks and Oliver, a CBBC magazine. He loved his books despite his young age, and would point to things and say the name of it, and absolutely loved *In The Night Garden*, a children's program on CBBC. Whilst in the shop browsing, I had to look at the magazines—I just had to have something to absorb all of the time, my brain never shuts down. I have to be learning, and by this time the music was fettling out, and I was no longer in a band. I happened to find a ***Beginner's Guide To Excel***. I bought it and studied it on the train while Joshua slept and Oliver looked at his magazine. I studied that book on our return too, and I practiced and learnt. I **loved** Excel. This was so cool. It wasn't just a calculator; I could write these codes called formulas and do all sorts of things. I could colour code stuff, sort stuff—it was amazing and so satisfying, like the feeling I had with those art sets.

Within six weeks, I was teaching my Manager Martin, the Senior Traffic Dispatcher, how to use Excel and coming up with some great solutions for work. He looked at me one day and said, **"You made a good impression of being thick all those years."** I took it as a compliment but also felt a little bit angered by it.

The Internal Conflict

I started to share this info with others in the business, and suddenly the Depot Manager called me into the office. He said he was loving what I was doing, but I was not to contact other branches, and I was to copy him into every email I sent going forwards. I did just that. I wanted to show him I could do exactly what he said; I wanted to impress him. A week or so later, he invited me to apply for the Employee Development Programme where I would go on training courses and learn all about running a depot. He also wanted me to do some HR courses. I was delighted; this was great, I was getting recognised. I was so proud of how I was doing. I even decided that as my Manager had brought all of his awards from other businesses and had them on a shelf in his office, I would bring in mine from the tyre company and display it on my desk. Yep, thinking back, that wasn't a great idea. He wasn't impressed and said I should take it home as it wasn't from that company, but neither were his awards and that just didn't feel right to me, there was a sense of injustice. At the same time, he was putting more and more on my Manager Martin, and you could see the stress building. He was being called into the Depot Manager's Office a lot. He was starting to struggle. I just kept my head down and carried on and took up the slack as much as I could. I then developed ways of working better using Excel and could take on more.

Eventually my Manager left, his mental health had just declined to the point he couldn't do it anymore—no warning, he just disappeared—and the Depot Manager immediately promoted me to Senior Traffic Dispatcher. I felt really sorry for him as I knew exactly what this felt like. The guys that were still driving really didn't like it; they saw me as the enemy now. It was a real them-and-us culture. I just wanted to do my best work though and make the manager proud. I felt like he was coaching me; he would often call as he was off of the site a lot and make me go in the yard and talk to him on the traffic office mobile handset. He wanted to know everything everyone was doing all of the time; he was relentless. I started to discover that things weren't right and noticed that the weights weren't correct when looking at the data as the drivers had to weigh each bin on the dustcart. I kind of knew what was happening. Many times, they would just drive past a job and jolt on the brakes to get a weight to save it down on the onboard scales, cheating the system. They would be emptying some of the bins only once a fortnight if they knew they could get away with it. This way they would get away with only doing three-quarters of their round each day and as it was job and finish, they could go home early. I hated it. I always wanted to do things right. In fact, I was often the last one back in the yard and all the others had gone home when I was driving. It used to wind me up as I knew they were cheating, I always had to do things right. I decided that if I wanted to be a depot manager one day and I was aware of this, I must say something. The Depot Manager wasn't interested and told me to never repeat it again, I didn't until now. As long as the work was done he was happy, and he was giving the guys more and more work—work I knew wasn't manageable—but they were getting pats on the back as the figures were getting better and better.

The "Cool Blue" Revelation

Things were going well on the Management Development Programme, and I was learning about profitability. They had a half-day session on looking at the profit and loss account of a depot—my first glimpse of **Management Accounts**. I loved it. I had always been good with money; this was great. I came up with loads of **cost-saving** ideas we could use too. One week we were given a homework task. I had some great ideas and decided to share them with the team. To me, that's what it was about—all helping each other for the good of the business. As requested, I copied my Manager in like I was told to; every single email he was copied in on without fail. The next day, he called me into the office and told me under no circumstances must I ever help other people on the course and that the trainer had complained about me. I tried to say that I wanted to help others, but he cut me short and told me if I did it again I would be in big trouble. I felt sick. I hated doing anything wrong; I just cowered down and did what he said. A week later I apologised to one of the trainers for doing so, telling him my manager had put me straight. He was bemused. He said, "Teamwork is what it's all about. Just carry on, I'll speak to him."

Another day on the course, we were doing something called **Insights**. You had to answer 50 questions online about what you would do in certain situations at work, and the day of the course they delivered us a booklet. It had graphs and lots of words. In it, it told us about our personality. I was shocked and amazed. It knew how my brain worked. It knew my most inner thoughts. It knew about my self-doubt, my social anxiety, my struggle with building relationships, my desire to do everything right and stick to the rules, my need for researching everything, and even how I absorbed information. How can they find out so much? They seem to know more about me than Kerry. I was truly astounded, I was just gobsmacked, these were my deepest secrets. Apparently I was a **'Cool Blue'**; I was a person that needed detail. They were right. I would spend hours learning the minutest of detail for obsessions. If I was to buy anything, I would do hours of research before I made a decision.

Later that day, they had us all standing up in a row, and they were to ask us questions and depending on the answer we took a step left or a step right. This was fun. We all lined up. On the first question we all moved different ways. The second one I moved to the left; most others moved right. By the end of the series of questions, I was right up against the wall as far as I could have gone, and, **all alone**. Everyone else was around the middle or across the other side. ***Why was I so different?***

We were told that those to the right of the centre were **extroverts**; they were people that were the life and soul of the party, the fun ones, and they would be the ones that talk first and think afterwards. Anyone on the left was an **introvert**; we were the quiet ones. We would think first and then talk. They were right. I would have conversations in my head practising what I would say to someone. I did it constantly. Then I would replay it after, kicking myself because I didn't say what I wanted to say. These words were new to me. Why had no one ever explained introverts and extroverts to me? For many years I thought I was broken. I didn't want to go out many times. Often I didn't want to talk, and yes, I thought about things for hours and hours. My brain never switched off. I had always thought I was a bit different and didn't quite fit in; now there was a word for it.

The Final Collapse

I continued in the office, but the Manager was starting to be tougher and tougher on me. I kept trying everything to please him. One day we had a driver shortage due to illness. I took a dustcart out, drove for nine hours, and completed a whole round. Then I came back to the office and completed my job. I worked over 17 hours that day. I was expecting a huge pat on the back. Nothing. It got worse and worse, and the Manager was speaking to me quite badly. I was just like a scared puppy though and just jumped and did what he said. I feel quite ashamed at how fragile I was back then, despite being a truck driver. I certainly didn't fit the stereotype. This was my chance to prove myself. I couldn't let him down. If he was angry with me, there must be a reason. Maybe I am a bit useless, just like my teachers and parents told me. This started to get me down.

One day I walked in and he shouted at me, **"This carpet is disgusting, get the fucking hoover out!"** I did it straight away. *What had I done? Why was he so angry?* That weekend I came into the office and completely blitzed it, pulled the cupboard out, and reorganised it. I just wanted to prove myself. I gave my weekend up for free, just to try and please. Whatever I did, it just got worse. My mental health was getting really bad, and I was at the point I couldn't take any more. It got so bad that I took a **USB recorder** to the office in the top pocket of my shirt and recorded him so I could ask Kerry what she thought. Kerry was disgusted and wanted to go and see him. Now, that would have been embarrassing. I couldn't take it any more, and eventually I got ill, just like the time at the Tyre and Exhaust Centre. The brain fog was immense. I couldn't get out of bed in the morning, and I was just in a big dark hole. Kerry told me that she thought he felt threatened by me. I totally dismissed it. I mean, **I'm a stupid ex-binman with no GCSEs**. Why on earth would this guy who had won multiple awards feel **threatened** by me?

Chapter 11 - Down Like A Sack Of Spuds

The Final Breakdown

I woke up one morning. I could no longer function. I was a broken man, again; I just couldn't get out of bed. Kerry phoned in for me; I just couldn't speak to my Manager. He was being so horrid to me. I was signed off by the doctor. **Why was this happening to me again and again? Why was I so weak? Why did everyone dislike me?**

After a couple of weeks, I had a conversation with HR. I explained the issue, and they said I needed to raise a grievance, go back to work, or hand in my notice. I knew in this state I wouldn't get another job, but I just couldn't work with him any more. I couldn't afford to quit either; we were now fully working to a tight budget. I had no choice but to raise a grievance but I hated the thought of that. I really didn't do well with conflict; it would physically impact me. I knew I would be okay, though, as I had the recording, but I still felt sick to the stomach.

A letter arrived for me to attend a meeting at a nearby depot. I felt sick with anxiety all the way there. I was terrified. I didn't really want to do this at all, but I needed a job. I also really couldn't work with the guy any more. I walked through the office as fast as I could as I really didn't want to speak to the colleagues there. I knew I had such brain fog and just felt again like **I was on the inside looking out,** like I was there but not a part of it, trapped inside my body. I went up to the office, and there were three people from HR: one to interview me, one to take notes, and one as a witness. They were one side of the desk; I was the other. There was a desk separator between them that we had to look over to talk to each other. They asked me how I was and then asked me to explain my grievance. I tried as best I could, but it was like what I was saying was just jumbled up words. I wasn't in a great place. I suggested they listen to the audio files I had sent them. They listened to the audio files, asked me a few questions, and then asked me to wait outside. I waited outside for what seemed like ages, massive butterflies in my stomach and physically shaking. They came out. They said that they agreed the manager had been unprofessional, but they were withholding the grievance, and I should either return to work or give them my notice. I couldn't return. I just gave them my notice.

Back to Black

I was in a terrible state. I was broken, but I had to fix this. I had children and a wife; we couldn't survive for long. I worked hard on getting myself better. I had done this before; I knew I just had to rest and eat well. Kerry was there, but she was also working, so I had to still get the kids to the babysitter. The Doctor had given me access to some online courses called **CBT (Cognitive Behavioural Therapy)**. I was working through these, and the fog was starting to clear in my mind. I had to get on and sort my head out as money was getting short, and we were now at the point of using credit cards.

I decided I wanted to not go back to driving but to have another go at management. I desperately wanted those happy days again that we had in the branch I had turned around. I knew that doing something like this, if I got the right place and the right people would positively impact my mental health and I knew I could do it. I wanted to get back into the tyre trade. I had missed it. I had made great friends there, something I had never done since.

I looked for several jobs, and one looked great. It was a **Manager's** job working for an established, family-run tyre business. The owner's wife was interviewing. She had noted how the company was very old fashioned; she wanted to help her husband bring it up to scratch, modernise it, and boost sales. The interview was in a lovely country hotel, and there was the owner's wife and a woman who ran a recruitment business, who happened to be her best friend. The interview was fantastic. They were such lovely ladies, and I told them of my desire to do better for myself, how I was a previous **Manager of the Year** in the tyre trade, and how I had that buzz again and wanted to better myself. The job sounded great: trying to build the business up. I was excited. I knew I could do this. There were four parts to the business: a breakdown and tyre replacement service for trucks, just like at Magnum Tyres; scrap tyre processing with tyres going off to Africa as part-worn tyres; a small truck tyre wholesale; and a small-scale remould production using two big autoclaves—big pressure sealed ovens that cure the rubber. I'd even get a company van. The next stage was a call with the owner. We seemed to get on well, and we even had people in common—in fact, the owner knew all of the team from Magnum Tyres. To my absolute surprise, I got the job. The money was great too and a massive step up, almost as much as I was earning as a driver. I said I would start the following week, just so I could fully prepare myself.

During that week, I was asked to go and pick up some overalls as I would be needing them. I went to the supplier and got measured, but they couldn't supply me as the account was on stop. I had to call my new boss and explain. He wasn't happy; told me to wait while he made some phone calls and he'd get me served. Sure enough, I got the overalls. My stomach did start to churn though—was this just an error or was the business in a bad place?

The Toxic Trade

I started the very next week; it was August 2014. I was thrown straight into loading up trucks with truck tyres. I thought, *ahh, maybe they are just busy*. It appeared though that the husband, and owner of the business, had no thoughts about modernisation or improving the business. It was fine just as it was. He just wanted a **right-hand man**, one that could just oversee things and answer the phone and load vehicles while he was out in a truck collecting scrap tyres. This was different to what I had been told. It turned out there was no company vehicle either—that was a mistake! I really wasn't happy. I spent most of my days lifting truck tyres, and my back really wasn't enjoying it.

The culture there was horrid too. The owner's sister seemed to be the boss, and she, the accounts girl, and the admin lady were very **cliquey**. I hated spending time there. The sister was also very, very abrupt. I constantly felt on edge. There were so many issues too: no real health and safety, the team were unhappy, the tachograph documentation wasn't in line with regulation—it was terrible—and the conditions the guys worked in were appalling. They had lunch in a mouldy portacabin with a rotten floor. I tried to build rapport and get the guys on side. They didn't like the gloves they used and were buying their own. The ones supplied by the business, they had to sign for and they were not allowed to be chucked away until the owner of the business agreed they were worn out, but they were damp and really stunk. I contacted the company that supplied them and made a deal where we could get the gloves the guys liked for cheaper than the ones we were buying. It was **win-win**; the guys would be happy and the company would save money. The owner didn't share the same views however. He raised his voice at me: **"I know what gloves are best and that's what we are using, end of."** I started to realise this wasn't going to be the place for me, I wasn't prepared to make myself ill again, it was time to think about doing something new.

The Accounting Epiphany

I thought long and hard about what I could do. Nothing was working. I was succeeding and failing and just getting nowhere fast; it was just such a roller coaster. Often during my working day I'd go and sit in the cold outside toilet—we could only use that one, the indoor one was for the women—or I'd sit in the warehouse, anything to keep out of the toxic atmosphere in the office. I started to think about all the jobs I had done in the past, what I liked about them, what I didn't like about them, and also about what I learnt about the way I think. I researched it, put it all together, and over the coming weeks did some research on what I should do.

One freezing cold day, sitting in the outside toilet, I searched for **'careers for cool blue introverts in an office, no weekends.'** A few different jobs came up: a **Data Scientist**, a **Graphic Designer**—no, that wasn't me. Then, I saw **Accountant**. I felt a smile. Could this be it? Could I become an Accountant? No. But..hmmm...maybe. I liked the idea, just I had no idea how I would ever achieve that in my wildest dreams.

I researched a lot. I was a **Cool Blue**, of course! I started to think, yes, it's almost impossible, but I can't go on in life being this unhappy, I have to try. I needed a course I could do at home. No one in their right mind would employ me as an Accountant. I hadn't got a GCSE to my name and, to be honest, most bosses seemed to think I was useless, just like my teachers and parents did. But I knew deep down I could do more. If only someone would give me a chance, if only I could find **MY** people. I wanted to prove I wasn't this good-for-nothing man quickly approaching middle age. I thought, if I could start to get some qualifications, then maybe, just maybe I could work as an assistant in an office and start from there.

I researched some more and found that there were two different types of accountants: **Financial Accountants** and **Management Accountants**. Financial Accountants did the mandatory reporting and tax and reported on everything that had happened before, whereas Management Accountants focused on the future, business growth, strategy, pricing. This excited me. I knew that, I had grown a business before and it gave me a fantastic buzz. I researched some more and found **CIMA, The Chartered Institute Of Management Accountants**. This seemed like exactly what I wanted to do. I was so excited and it sounded so posh and prestigious. I could even get letters after my name—that's what those really intelligent people do that go to university. Wow, I would be so proud; I'd make Kerry and the kids proud too.

But then I thought, *actually, come on, I'm useless*. Who the hell would give me a job as an Accountant? I ran it past Kerry. She said I should go for it. I said, **"Really?"** She said, **"Yes, I believe in you, babe. I know you can do it."** We were skint though, and most of it my fault for being a failure. If I did this, it had to be everything to me. I'd have to dedicate myself. I spoke to my Dad, and he agreed to lend me £1,000 towards my first course.

The First Exam

I started to research courses and found a company that could supply an online version of the course. There were four exams to sit, and this would be the certificate level. Once completed, I would have a '**Certificate in Business Accounting**'. Once I had completed that, there were another 12 exams to sit, three of which would be three-hour case studies. This was going to be one hell of a task! I booked the first course; it was on **Business Economics** and started immediately. *Ahh, no, what have I done?* I felt lost, sick. I just didn't understand a lot of it. I didn't even know how to use a calculator to find a square root. What an idiot. *What was I thinking in trying to do this? I couldn't even pass a GCSE and this course would be what* *some people did after university.* I'd now borrowed money from my Dad though; I couldn't just go back and say sorry, it's too hard. I had to find a way.

I found some books from the **'Dummies Guide'** series online: one on Bookkeeping, one on Financial Accounting, and another on Management Accounting. I read some samples and I seemed to understand it better. These books were written for someone like me, a dummy! So I ordered them and waited for them to arrive. I also bought a book called *The Economics Book* by DK Publishing.

The books were great. In fact, they are still on the bookshelf in my office where I'm writing this book. Not just those books: there are four floor-to-ceiling bookshelves, all full of books and hardly a story book in sight. The only ones there belong to Kerry. I'll talk more about my books later and how I amassed so many. I would go back and forth between the books to get a basic understanding and then back to the **CIMA** course to take it up a notch, occasionally watching a YouTube video too if I just couldn't grasp it. Passing this exam was like another **'guitar in the window'** moment—it got me through horrendous days of stacking truck tyres and dealing with a toxic atmosphere.

I slogged on for a couple of months. It was slow going, but it took my mind off work and gave me focus. It was still a nightmare there. I hated it. It was now November 2014. The drive there and back was long and in the dark, and the weather almost as cold as the vibe in the office. I did manage some great things there though. I managed to rearrange the warehouse and make it safer. I built up some wholesalers, and I got their driver and vehicle records all in order, despite me once finding out the owner was driving a truck around London without a valid licence. That was a panic. There was a lot going on that I didn't want to be a part of. I liked doing things right and I followed rules. I decided I needed to look for another job. It was getting so toxic there I just didn't want to make myself ill again. It got to a point where enough was enough, and I handed in my **three months notice**. Then another shock came: the owner's father, who originally started the business, offered to pay me in cash each month if I stayed. That was it. I was absolutely out of there!

Just a week before Christmas and it was dragging me down working my notice. I hated every minute there. Then one evening, the women in the office started on me. The accounts girl called me a **"fucking twat."** I looked over at the owner's sister. She really didn't seem bothered. That was it. I marched over, slammed my keys and work phone on the desk and said, **"That's it, I'm done. I just can't stand another minute in this place."** I only returned once more, to hand back my overalls and gloves!

Triumph and Desperation

I was now in a really bad place financially, however, I had made the decision to leave before I had made myself ill this time. Money was tight. Christmas was here, and I had no job and was trying to study. Kerry and I spoke, and Kerry agreed that she would work extra hours and I was to get these first exams completed to give me a chance of getting a job that would give me a better opportunity. Kerry knew it would be a struggle, but she didn't want to see me ill again either.

I studied hard, also keeping an eye on the job market, but the main aim was to get some exams passed. I was now ready to pass my first one. I was booked in at a local test centre. The exam was multiple choice on a computer. I was so nervous. I felt sick, but I knew I had just one chance at this. I couldn't afford to not pass. I had worked hours and hours for this. But then on the other hand, *I was useless.* Everyone had told me this for most of my life. *What was I doing?* My mind was doing somersaults along with my belly.

I went in, my palms clammy, my heart racing, trying to keep my head clear and not let it fog up. I sat down. I felt sick. I popped the headphones on, read the instructions, and then, this was it. When I hit the next button, the exam would start. The tension was horrendous. I hit the button and I was off. My first exam since school, and I was now 38. I answered as many questions as I could. I felt I had done well. Then, taking the advice I read, anything I was unsure of I took a guess. Time was tight, and I just about got an answer in for everything. I nervously took off my headphones and returned through the door to the office, my heart was beating so hard I was almost breathless, trembling at the knees, patiently waiting to be called over for my result. They called my name out. I went over, expecting to see written on the paper what people had reinforced in my head my whole life over: **FAILURE**. I shakily took the paper, opened it up carefully, and it said **PASS**.

I felt myself welling up. *I did it, I did it!* I was so damn happy. I couldn't believe I had passed an Accountancy exam—me, that failure that was good for nothing but a building site according to school. I wanted to jump up and down. I was dizzy with happiness. I couldn't thank the lady in reception enough. I grabbed my stuff and headed out of the door with urgency. I needed to tell Kerry and my Dad. **"I passed, I passed, I passed!"** I shouted down the phone, Kerry and **I** jumping up and down, tears of happiness in my eyes. I drove home that day with absolute pride and celebrated with my little family.

The Momentum

My Dad was so pleased and offered to pay for the next course to help me out. The very next day I booked it. This one was on **Financial Accounting**. I already had my Dummies guide, and I was away—let's get this one done. I studied so hard, and within just a matter of weeks I felt I was ready. I headed to the test centre again, still nervous, but this time, it was a little more familiar. I still had the nerves, I still had the negative thoughts, but I did it again: another one in the bag.

This was it. I had passed two accounting exams, but I had failed my maths GCSE. How was this possible? Had I just gained more intelligence as I got older? It just seemed different. It wasn't like school. I could **hyperfocus** in silence, and if I struggled, I could walk away and have a break. I could just do ten minute stints if I wanted, or sometimes in hyperfocus it just flowed and I'd study all day with hardly a break. Money was getting tight now though, and I had to start thinking about work. I couldn't just be a student at my age and have my Dad pay for my courses. I had to get a job. I didn't want any job though. I wanted a job that would give me a chance, an opportunity, a job where I might be able to start at the bottom and realise my dream of becoming an Accountant.

The Covert Interview

I started to think about companies that had head offices based near to where we were living now. There were three major ones: a building society, a credit card company, and a builders' merchant. I found a suitable job in all three and applied for them all. The mortgage company one was an analyst; I heard nothing back. The credit card company was for a fraud analyst; I got offered the job online, but through an Agency. The builders merchant one was for a Branch Manager. I had Management experience, albeit a long time ago. I got an interview. This was it, my big chance.

As part of the pre interview process, I was given some profit and loss figures, and I was to create a five-year plan for the branch. My first plan of attack was to get to know the business. I popped on some old jeans and a hoody and went to the branch. I posed as a customer wanting some prices for landscaping products for a business I was thinking of setting up after being made redundant. The story was that I was going around local builders' merchants to get prices and was working out the viability of starting up on my own. I went in, a little nervous but tried to play it cool. I never had the social mobility issues with stuff like this, just a few nerves. I think it was because I had an agenda, I wasn't having to rely on just small talk. I stood there for about 10 minutes, totally ignored. Finally, someone served me. I got prices printed out for a **tonne bag of plum slate chippings**, a **tonne bag of gravel**, and some **railway sleepers**. They gave me a price, didn't ask about my project or why I wanted a price, and didn't take any details. This was a missed opportunity. Either that, or they had sussed me out as a hopeless fake.

I went home and got to work preparing my plan. I felt so good about this. I knew the structure of the management accounts and how they worked. I could see the numbers that needed to change and knew just how I could change them, I could visualise it all. It was all about customer service and following up leads. Had I been there that day, I would have acknowledged every single customer, not after ten minutes, but as soon as they caught my eye. If I was busy, I would ask them politely if they would mind waiting, I would be with them next. Always make the customer feel welcome, value their time, and make them feel at ease. After all, without customers we don't have a business. This is what I was taught in my tyre days. Next up, follow the lead. How could they tell if I had started a business up? How could they know if I was either a lone landscaper pricing up a one off job or one with a whole army working for me and I was shopping around? Without asking, they would never know. Without taking my details, they could never follow it up. As soon as I walked out of that door, I was a lost customer. Not only that, I was a lost customer that had just cost them money on time, paper, electricity—there was absolutely no return on that investment. You might think that the cost there is minimal, say £2 for someone's time, 1p for the ink, 5p for the paper and 1p for the electricity and wear and tear on the paper. That's £2.07p. You might not think that's a lot but then think, if your profit margin, what you make out of the total sale, is 10% then that's £20.70 worth of sales you need to generate to pay for that interaction. Let's multiply that up, a very conservative 4 customers per day in a branch, that's now £82.80. Now let's build it up, there are 252 trading days in a year, say this happened on half of them, we now have £10,432.80 as the cost of not following up leads just in that branch, not to mention the sales lost to competitors. Now multiply that up to 600 branches and you can see just how impactful it is to acknowledge customers. Added to this, there is the reputation: builders, in the majority, are very social, they will talk and eventually that leads to more missed sales from customers that never even contact you.

A Foot in the Door

I researched thoroughly for the interview. I knew about the long history of the company, how many branches they had. I absorbed everything I could. I headed to the **Regional Office** for my interview. I was prepared, confident, but still absolutely nervous. The site was huge, trucks going in and out, a large branch, an office, a tool hire branch, and a plumbing and heating branch, all there together. I'd been there so many times before, but that was in a truck, emptying the bins. I was hoping I had the right part. I waited by a great wooden staircase in the middle of a large reception. There was some more information on the wall about the business. I stood there and absorbed it and went over my notes.

The Regional Manager came down the stairs and invited me up to his little cubby hole office overlooking the yard. He was really down to earth. We did the introductions and he asked me a few questions, then asked me to present my plan. Then he asked me about my experience in the trade. I had none. That was it. *Was this the end?* He said he was very impressed with me, but that the advert was for one of their larger branches and wouldn't be suitable for anyone without a lot of experience in the trade. I felt deflated. He paused, **"But……I like you. I like what you have done and your observations in that branch. I'm going to give you a chance,"** he said. My face lit up! He said that the branch next to us needed someone that could work the stock as they were about to have a huge refit. He also wanted someone that could step up and run transport to cover for holidays and that I had a great experience in my driving and traffic dispatching days. He suggested I could take this on as a sort of Branch Manager Designate and go from there after building up some experience. He invited me to go and see the Manager there and then in the branch over the road.

I went over with the Regional Manager and waited a while while he went into the **Manager's** office. He came out and said, **"He's just with a customer at the minute. I've had a word with him about you. If he likes you, we might just have a job for you."**

I waited nervously, watching what went on in the busy branch, taking it all in, how people behaved, how they spoke. I was checking to see if I could blend in. The Manager called me in and we spoke for a while. We seemed to get on well. He said, **"I'll tell you what, leave it with me. If I can make this work, I'll get back to you."**

The next week I got a phone call, **"You can start next month if you like. You'll be working on our branch refit. You can start in February."** I was over the moon. They had over 30,000 staff and the head office was in the same town. This could be my chance. I knew that time was now precious and that I had to sit another exam before I started my new job. Dad couldn't lend me any more money but I had to get this done. I had no choice, I had to use a credit card. I couldn't just sit around and waste time. I booked the course. This one was on **Business Ethics and Business Law**.

Law and Latin

I was lost! Again, *no, what had I done?* I had to learn Latin phrases such as **"Ad Valorem," "Bona Fide"** among others, and learn, and be examined on, British Case Law such as **Pharmaceutical Society of Great Britain v Boots Cash Chemists (Southern) Ltd [1953] EWCA Civ 6**. In this famous case, the claimant, the Pharmaceutical Society of Great Britain, argued that the display of a product with a price was an offer, which a customer accepted by placing the item in their basket. Because certain medicines needed to be sold under the supervision of a registered pharmacist, they argued that Boots was breaking the law since the "sale," the formation of the contract, happened when the customer took the item from the shelf, unsupervised. The defendant, Boots, successfully argued that the display of goods was merely an **invitation to treat**. The customer makes the offer to purchase when they take the goods to the till. The shop assistant, in this case, supervised by a pharmacist for the regulated items, then accepts the offer at the till, and that's when the contract is formed. The court sided with Boots, establishing that a sale in a self-service store is completed at the checkout, not at the shelf. Just like a self service checkout in a supermarket when they have to authorise your alcohol or medicines.

Now, can you imagine a guy that not long ago was driving a dustcart or transporting sewage, hardly went to school and didn't collect his GCSE results, and was constantly told he was useless, having to do this? Again, I felt sick with worry. But I knew, if I could just find a way of absorbing it, and I really took an interest in it, I could do this. That was it, I needed more books. This time I **bought *Essentials Of Business Law* by Ewan MacIntyre**, ***Lawyers' Latin* by John Gray**, and a tatty old copy of the ***Oxford Law Dictionary***. Again, they all sit on my shelf now and are still a source of information.

I worked so hard, every hour I could, hyper-focusing and absorbing every word I could consume. Again, I turned up at the test centre nervous, belly doing somersaults, but adamant I had to pass this exam. I sat there, mouth dry, tapping my legs, taking a final deep breath before pressing the button to start the exam. Again, I answered everything I knew and flagged anything I didn't or anything I just struggled with, and went back to it at the end, I just about managed to get it all done. That time came again: walking out into the reception, nothing more I could do, nothing more I could give. This was it. I couldn't afford failure either financially or time-wise.

I opened the paper with apprehension. This one was tough. **PASS** it read. I was delighted! The lady I had come to know and knew my back story was delighted. That was it. I had to get down those stairs and outside so I could tell Kerry. **"I passed, I passed!"** I said. Kerry was as happy as me. **"I told you you could do it. Believe in yourself,"** she said. I called my Dad. He was in disbelief. "You passed? What? You did it?"

"Yes," I said, **"I bloody did it! This ex-binman is going to be an accountant."**

Chapter 12 - Building Up

Order from Chaos

It was February 2015, and my first day at the builders' merchants. I got some uniform, had a tour, and for the most part of the day sat on a laptop doing an induction. It was an okay day; everyone seemed fairly friendly. There was a bit of a 'club' though: they hung out in the back office—the Assistant Manager, the admin lady, and some students that worked there part-time. The place was a dump. I'd have been shot in the national tyre chains if my branch looked like this. In the corner of the stock room was a huge pile of goods—just chucked on the floor, all sorts of tools and ironmongery. It looked like something I had just tipped out of the back of a truck. I didn't say much; it wasn't my place to. I just went with the flow, but it bugged me a lot. I hated disorder; everything had to have its place, just like those stationery sets as a child. Within a week the refit started. Well, if I thought there was a mess already, it was about to get worse, much worse.

The branch had to continue trading but also had to have a major refit in store. You could see why. I know it was a builders' merchant, but it was a dump. None of the shelves matched. Stock was just bundled on shelves; nothing seemed to be in a logical place. There would be dumps of excess stock thick with dust on the floor. **How on earth could they stocktake this?** The rip out started. It was like one of those puzzles you had as a kid—you know, those little plastic ones with the squares that made a picture where one square was missing so you could move them around in the frame until you got them in order.

I spent my days covered in dust and grime moving shelves of paint, plumbing parts, taps, nails, screws, and ironmongery that looked like it had been there for years. We had a mezzanine area, but that was full of every type of door you could think of: fire doors, french doors, plain doors, patterned doors, all sorts of sizes, all of the wrappers ripped and covered in dust, stacked on pallets. Alongside this, pallet upon pallet of old stock with thick layers of dust. I worked tirelessly with the refit team, merchandisers, and category managers from head office. I loved putting things in order, all brand new shelving that matched, cleaning the dust off, putting stock in logical order, perfectly aligned in the shelf in rows like soldiers, just like my days back at the fishing tackle shop. It was so satisfying.

I had a thought though as the team put up the new shelving that went left to right across the long shop floor. Why was it this way? You couldn't see down the aisles and watch customers to see if they needed help with a purchase and, more to the point, you couldn't see if anyone was stealing anything. This was also made easier by having clip strips (you know, the ones you see hanging on supermarket shelves with pork scratchings and the like on) that had carrier bags on with catalogues in and little white paint kettles—just the perfect containers for thieves. I brought it up, but this was the plan. This was the blueprint for all branches, and it was a set up that worked. I cracked on. Maybe they had researched it. They were professionals, they must know. It just didn't make logical sense to me though.

For almost a month this work continued. I wasn't happy with the pile of stock still on the floor though. I took it upon myself to use the old racking in the open space in the stock room—somewhere to put the over stocks, of which there were plenty. I couldn't just erect shelves though and put stock on it, my head didn't work like that. I colour coded every shelf for different categories: an area for paint, one for electrical, one for plumbing etc. The shelves put lengthways with room for a person and a trolley between each row, all perfectly aligned. I created a coding system too, and in Excel I colour coded cells and added a key to make a map of the exact layout and stated the rules of stock put away and printed them out and put them on the wall. I also created a policy of keeping the doors shut at all times to avoid theft. I was very anal about this. Many people didn't care: **"It's just a store room. Just whack it on a shelf"** was the attitude. It infuriated me. To me it was just so logical and easy and saved time—why couldn't others see? It was like back in the days of the tyre branch where I was a Manager. I just knew that if we had things organised and to hand it would save time, reduce customer waits, ensure we knew where stock was, and enable more accurate stock-taking. They had a system here the same as the tyre trade, a cyclical stock take where you had a range of items each day to check off. There was a routine set of products that went in logical order, but also anything that had gone into a negative quantity too, of which there were many.

The Rugby Star

It was in this branch that I also grew a love for Rugby, through sheer embarrassment! My manager was talking to a giant of a customer—this bloke had some huge shoulders on him. He called me over, **"Gav can you help this chap, he's just been given a nail gun by a supplier. It's a new one on the market, can you call them and get some nails for him, they'll know who he is?"**

"No problem," I said. **"What's your name mate?"**

My Manager looked at me in absolute disbelief. **"It's Tom Wood, England Captain. You don't follow Rugby do you."**

"No," I said embarrassingly, and slid off to the office feeling like a right idiot. It turns out Tom had been sharing his love of woodwork on social media and the company had sent him one of their new nail guns. It worked out well though as just a week later I actually got to see him play when a few of us were offered free tickets as part of a team building night out. I've been a rugby fan ever since and many years later even ended up coaching an under-12s team that my son played in. I knew nothing about the rules and still don't know much, but I loved the game and learnt as much as the kids; my part was all about mindset and encouragement, something I came to learn lots about over the following years.

Stock Accuracy: My Mission

Back to the builders merchants', and eventually, after about six months, in July 2015, they unofficially made me **Branch Stock Manager**. I would do the ordering, the stock-taking, and put the stock away, along with another guy that also did that. It was probably so they could shove me in the back office out of the way to be honest. I was a bit of a nerd about stock at this point. I loved it. My own office out the way. I was on a mission. I wanted to make an impact, as this was my chance to try and get my first job in a real office. I had to make a name for myself. I researched. I learnt everything I could about stock and used my recent CIMA knowledge from my business economics course to make a difference.

The first thing to attack was all those negative stocks. I started to investigate exactly why they were negative. I wasn't happy just adjusting them to 1 only to do the same again at a later date. I then started to think about why it had happened, what was causing it—mainly it was paperwork not being handed in to the office and the goods not being booked in. This then created stock to sell, but it wasn't on the system and hence when it was sold, the stock quantity went to a negative number, people would just book it out and not question why. I communicated around the branch and sent team emails out to ensure that all paperwork was handed in and not left on the back of a forklift or attached to the goods. I also kept a log so I could see the patterns of which suppliers or which staff member took the goods in so I could then address the issues. It was hard work. Not everyone was that bothered; they just saw me as a pain in the backside. In fact, one day one of them said, **"Why are you working here? Why don't you just chill, fuck 'em. I just come here to earn my money and go home."** I didn't think like that at all. I really cared. This meant so much to me. I wanted to be seen. I wanted to make a difference. I actually really cared, and I got a great deal of satisfaction every time I improved something.

The negative stock was getting better, but I had to tackle the next thing: ordering. The ordering system was an old MS DOS system from the 1980's—it was horrific! I decided I would find a way to download the stock data and analyse it in a spreadsheet. I did it. This was great. I could see negative stocks in an instant by filtering the quantity to less than zero, all there in one place. I could add a column to the spreadsheet with a formula that looked at the quantity versus the minimum required quantity. I could see how often they sold and what the minimum order quantities were. It gave me a wealth of information. I then started to act on the information. There would be so much to do, but each day between filling shelves and signing off deliveries, I would be there, in **hyperfocus** in the back office working my data. I loved it there, all quiet, no hustle and bustle, and I could make a real difference. I knew that if we didn't have the stock, we couldn't sell it. This was an important job.

Gradually the stock availability percentage increased as I was booking goods in on time and ordering goods before they ran out. I was anal with it. It was like a game to me; I had to complete it. I wanted 100%. It gave me a lot of satisfaction. However, there were some goods that, if I ordered the minimum amount of stock from the supplier, we would have about four years worth of stock. This is why we had piles of dusty stock. I couldn't do this, but I wanted that 100%. This was my little game. I like winning. *How could I do it?*

I had an idea: a collaboration. I would use the system to check those items of stock in branches in the local area. Low and behold, they had the same issue: either they had years worth of stock, or none at all. I had a plan. I phoned around the branches and arranged that if I ordered certain products, they would take a transfer of the products. Some were reluctant; they didn't even want them as they didn't really sell. They weren't bothered about stock availability. I did though. This was my mission. Eventually, I got some of the goods we needed in stock at decent quantities. Availability was now up to 98.7%—the highest in the region. I was winning. I had used my newly learnt skills to make a difference. Except no one really bothered or saw the point within the branch. However, I did get a 'well done' from a visiting Regional Director. That made my day. It made all that hard work worth it. At least someone recognised it. I absolutely loved being recognised. In fact, I think I craved it after years of being told I was useless. I wanted more! My next stop was dead stock. I created better clearance areas and created dead stock lists for the sales colleagues to try and get the stock moved on, and I continued to try and get stock housekeeping better, but buy-in wasn't great.

The Road to Head Office

At the same time this was going on, I was also covering for Transport occasionally. It didn't go well though. I would use the system to work out what to load on each of the lorries—there were five of them. Except the system had the wrong information on size and weight. I would get in a right muddle, and the drivers would get mad as they were overloaded. The thing is, I didn't know the products well enough or how they loaded on to the trucks in order to load and build effectively. It wasn't great. However, the transport manager was amazing at it. He was an absolute whizz, so when I took over, I'd get absolute shit off the drivers. I tried my best, but without the right data, and without the knowledge, I just couldn't do it like the Transport Manager. He was an ace.

Back to the stock, and there was a specialist team of three people based in an office over the road, looking at stock accuracy. I got to know them well as they would pop over to the branch to test things. Eventually they asked me to trial a new hand held stock taking device. I did, and I gave them feedback and helped them to fettle it. I was so obsessed with my stock, I used to talk about it with excitement. I loved what I did and I loved that I was getting results. The manager of the team of three said, **"I'll be working for you one day."** I took it that he was making fun of me. Most people did, to be honest. I thought he was trying to say that I was a bit over the top. He probably was; I still don't know. I certainly didn't think he was sincere. Not me. I was doing well here, but overall I was still a bit useless. I couldn't even sort the loading of a truck properly, I would always look at the negatives in myself.

One day we had someone come in from the head office. He wanted to know about stock and wastage and spoke about something called **Lean Six Sigma**. I had never heard of it, but apparently he was a Master Black Belt. Whatever that meant, it all sounded a bit like Karate to me. I was intrigued and wanted to learn more. I learnt that Lean Six Sigma was a business improvement tool that helps you cut waste from your business. Not waste as in the waste I was used to when driving trucks, but all sorts of waste. In fact, they had an analogy for it, **TIMWOOD**. This was also known as the 7 wastes and stood for **Transport, Inventory, Motion, Waiting, Overproduction, Overprocessing, and Defects**. I later learnt a new one to add: **Skills**. These were all areas you found wastage in business that reduced profitability. This got me interested. I totally got it. After the guy had explained it, I realised that what I had done in the tyre and exhaust branch as a manager was in fact Lean Six Sigma. I had removed the need to transport the wheels to the back of the garage to change the tyres. I had reduced waiting time for a ramp by creating more bays, and I had reduced defects by putting in procedures and quality control. To me this was common sense, and I saw waste all around me in the branch I was working at, certainly in inventory.

I was told that there were differing levels: white belt, yellow belt, green belt, and master black belt, and I was kind of right about thinking about Karate as this had its roots in Japan too, just like Karate does. Lean manufacturing was developed by Toyota just after World War Two. They called it **TPS,** the Toyota Production System, and it was a system that looked to eliminate waste, or **'muda'** in Japanese, from all aspects of production in order to give more value to the customer. It is still heavily used in many manufacturing businesses today. I was told that if I was interested there was a course coming up for colleagues and, if I delivered a project that saved the business £80,000, I would get a **green belt**. I took the guy's details and went home, and of course researched it. I loved it. I just totally got it. It was a qualification I could get that would show just what I could do. I spoke to my Manager and signed up the very next day. I chose a project on inventory waste, looking to eliminate damaged goods from the yard. There was plenty to go at.

A few months later, after being in the business for just 16 months, I was asked by the Manager of the project team if I would be interested in applying for a job at head office. They had heard what I had achieved with stock in the branch and wanted to create a brand new team of four **Branch Stock Improvement Managers** that would effectively do what I had touched on in the branch, but for all of the nearly 600 branches. Of course I was up for it. There was no stopping me. This was my chance to get a step closer to being an accountant. For the very first time, I would have a proper office job. I was asked to submit an application after talking to my Manager and to create a presentation answering two questions: **'Why is mandated stock availability in the branch important?'** and **'What are the main factors that impact our current availability performance?'** I know this as I still have it saved in my cloud drive. I went to work. I had learnt some presentation skills in the management development programme I had completed at the waste company.

Looking back, I noted that having high stock availability creates more sales in general, but also linked sales and impulse purchases by having certain items on display in certain areas. I noted that if the quantities were right and you kept an eye on the number of weeks your stock would last with average sales, you could also keep a buffer stock to try and reduce stock outs. I also spoke about brand perception and brand loyalty. I thought about how it would affect me as a customer if stock availability was poor. The main factors that impacted availability I knew like the back of my hand. I had lived it and breathed it: poor accuracy, poor housekeeping, excess lead times, high minimum order quantities, and lack of training. I delivered my presentation. I was trembling at the knees and just wanted to get out of the room, but I was confident I knew this stuff. I had been **hyper-focused** on it. I got the job! Just 16 months into the business I had gone from basically a shelf stacker to a **Branch Stock Improvement Manager**. You wouldn't believe how excited I was just to get a work laptop. I was so proud of it, yet nowadays I see it as no different than having a pen—it's a tool for a job—but to me back then it meant so much. I would just look at it and raise a smile. It may sound hilarious to some, but honestly, it was such a big deal.

Chapter 13 - Office Boy

Entering Head Office

In June 2016, I nervously met my team mates, got my pass to the building, and got to meet some of the people in the office, mainly the **supply chain** team, as that was our reporting structure. I was so nervous. I felt so unsure on what to say, who to speak to, how to act, how to dress—I worried about everything, I felt that I stood out like a sore thumb, it felt so awkward. I just didn't want to do or say the wrong thing and ruin it all as this was the big chance in my masterplan..

One of the team members was originally from Eastern Europe. This was a new thing to me. I had never worked with anyone that had come from another country before. I was apprehensive as to what to say, as in the previous working environments I had, they were certainly not diverse—far from it—and thinking back, the talk was basically racist, sexist, ableist, and just disrespectful. It was what I was brought up with all around me, at home, at school, at work, and even where I had just worked in the same business. I just wanted to be a nice person and be liked by everyone and I genuinely cared about everyone, but I was so scared of saying the wrong thing. I wanted to ask about his background and how he came to be here. I was genuinely interested in him, but so scared I might be seen as racist, intrusive, or disrespectful. I didn't want to be any of that.

The first week was really good. The four of us drove around the country visiting branches. It included a stay away too. Back at the office, we would mainly talk about ideas. We had nothing to follow; we were a new team. It was up to us to create the job description and write the rules. We had pretty much free rein and just the task to improve stock availability. We got on well. Two of us had worked in branches and made a difference with stock, one had worked at a distribution centre and again, was really into stock availability, one was from a supply chain background so looked at it from another angle. We gelled so well. We all had that joint passion for stock and stock availability; we were the super nerds. We even had our own separate space together in the large office. It felt like we were the **A**

Team, all absolutely driven in our purpose. I loved this; it was the first time I was in a job where everyone shared the same drive and passion to improve things.

The MBA Environment

Within a couple of weeks in the role, I was invited to some training: a Supply Chain course at Cranfield University, where we would have several two-day sessions. The first day we had an introduction, and then we spent some time in a lecture room: two massive interactive whiteboards, presentations, and a small case study. This was amazing. The whole **cohort** (another word that was new to me) was made up of colleagues from the same business, all from various areas of the supply chain.

At the end of the first day, we went off to our accommodation and were to meet in the bar to go for an evening meal with the lecturers. I was nervous, I had been fine talking shop in the lecture room but we were about to have no agenda. This was new. I was an ex-binman. I didn't speak their language. I didn't have their qualifications—in fact, I didn't have any really. I felt like I shouldn't be there, like I wasn't worthy. After meeting at the bar, we moved to a large room with the biggest table I had ever seen. I had people I had never spoken to before beside me and opposite. I was so scared to talk. This was way above me, and I had a university professor with an **MBE** sit near me. If I had a subject to talk about, an agenda, I was fine, this however, would be small talk, I was rubbish at it. This was a whole new environment. I felt privileged but out of my depth. I listened intently, tried to fit in with them, and add some insightful and intellectual sounding comments to the discussion, but I felt like a massive fake and I didn't want to sound stupid or less worthy of being there. I got through the evening, and the next day was better: more listening than talking, and an agenda.

I met a guy from one of our distribution centres that had also just started at head office. He originated from Poland. Again, I was so nervous talking with him. *What if I said the wrong thing?* It would take years for me to feel comfortable talking to people from other cultures. I was petrified of saying the wrong thing but was so interested as it was all new to me and in my previous world there was so much negativity. We learnt some amazing things about supply chain in those couple of days, some of which blew my mind, but it inspired another thirst for knowledge. I was starting to learn more, and it just made me want to expand on it further. I had found my passion, another obsession. Weekend reading would be text books on logistics, supply chain, inventory best practices—I absolutely absorbed everything.

Back at the office, and I was still nervous to speak up in meetings involving anyone other than our small team. Many had been to university. I was way inferior to them. There were Directors too, these were such important people, far superior to me. *What if I had a good idea and they thought it was stupid?* I couldn't spoil my chance here.

One day in a meeting with several directors in the **boardroom**, I sat there, nervous, hands clammy, absolutely busting to say something, but I couldn't. I was that scared kid in a room of adults again; I just couldn't talk. Afterwards, one of the directors asked me if I was OK as I was quiet. I said I was fine, I just didn't want to say the wrong thing, I was still new and was just taking things in. He gave me an excellent piece of advice that I still remind myself of today. He told me that I was there, not by chance, not by luck, but by hard work. I was there as the expert in the room, and that my ideas were just as valid as his or anyone else's in the room. It clicked. I still felt nervous, but from that day forward, I felt empowered to speak, worthy of being there, and had the permission I needed.

The Monopoly Game Project

As a team we did some amazing work together. We visited branches, warehouses, we mapped it all out, and we all knew that the main reasons for poor stock availability came down to poor systems and poor housekeeping. The issue was, how did we get people engaged like we were?

We hatched a plan. We needed it to be engaging, we needed it to teach people, we needed it to be specific to our systems. We created a game, based on the board game **Monopoly**. You would play it, as a group of branch managers, with your company laptop. Yes, your actual branch stock health, in real time, was part of the game. We created a mock up of the board, created chance cards with lost opportunities like losing a £500 sale as you didn't have the stock as it was incorrect on the system or you'd gained a sale of some dead stock that was on display near the counter and got a bonus £1000 sale. We got to writing scenarios. We had a stack of cards. We had different stops around the board where you would pick a card, and it would contain a question about your branch stock. You had to then use the suggested solution to go into your system and find the answer, in real time, and based on your answer you would either win or lose money for your branch. The money was to be fake with a picture of the CEO instead of the queen, all properly printed. The tokens were different bits of ironmongery or fittings. Everything was in theme and to be on brand. It was the game I was playing in my head in the branch. I loved winning and so many people do. This gamification would enable them to have the same feelings that I had around stock. We put it to our manager, presented it, and got them to play the game. They loved it! We ended up getting several sets made, and two of the team travelled the country for months playing the game with groups of branch managers. The feedback was amazing. People loved it. They were learning, sorting their stock out and understanding it in real time, but having fun doing it. They understood the reasons why good stock housekeeping was so important. The two of us remained at the office; we would look for the next project and also analyse the stock and see if our game was making a difference across the business.

The Power of Data

I was so passionate about this business and I was so determined to make a difference. However, I still had that issue with conflict, and emails were my preferred source of communication, especially if there was any element of conflict. My emails would be crazily long too. I had received no training on communication; I just wrote an email like I spoke in my head, but that was also different to how I spoke externally. Looking back, no wonder my communication wasn't effective. I remember once being called in the office about it and being told I had to change my communication style. I took some courses and learnt how to communicate much more effectively. I learnt that phrases such as **'as per my last email'** were actually seen as offensive. I just didn't get that; to me it was just a logical phrase. No one had taught me these unwritten rules. I got it in the end, but it didn't come easy.

With me now working in an office, the weight started to pile on. I was middle-aged and really started to worry about my health. I decided to do something I had never done since school and when I did do it at school, I hated it with a passion: running. I started with the **NHS couch to 5k app**, just running for around 30 second stints. It was hard, really hard. Some weeks I just couldn't complete it, but I was determined and I would just repeat the weeks until I managed them. As with everything in my life, I can't just do the standard stuff. I have to obsess, and this would become another obsession. I joined a running club. What I had noted was that it made me feel amazing afterwards. I hated turning up—all those people, no agenda, nothing to say, but by the time I'd finished, I just felt different. It helped me so much with my mental health. Within a year, I was now running **10 kilometres**, in just over an hour! I had also joined the club's cycling group, and we would ride once a week in the evening for up to 20 miles and at the weekend head out even further. Despite my teachers telling me I was an example of overnutrition, a couch potato, and once feeling like a fat lump, I went on to win runner of the year for my ability group two years running.

I did make myself look like a right wally at one point though. After a day in the office, I came home, loaded up the bike, and headed to our meeting point. We rode out in the rolling countryside for almost two hours. We had cycled well over 20 miles, heading towards 30. I hadn't learnt much about nutrition by then and hadn't eaten enough, so I started to get a bit shaky. We came to a stop at the traffic lights. Everyone unclipped their feet from the pedals and came to a stop. So did I, but without unclipping my feet from the pedals. It seemed like forever that I started to fall sideways, and just couldn't release my foot, and in what felt like slow motion, fell to the floor, still sat on and attached to the bike and all I could think about was not scratching my Garmin watch! What a complete idiot! I was so embarrassed. The guys could see I was a bit dazed and realised I probably had low sugar levels. They promptly got me some jelly babies. I sat on the verge for a while to get myself back on planet earth and headed sheepishly back to the car with the group.

Back at the office, the results were coming in: negative stocks went down, overdue orders went down, and stock availability continued to increase in many branches. The job, now we had this plate spinning, was to crack on with other projects. One project I turned back to was my **Lean Six Sigma Green Belt**. With my new found knowledge and wider sight on the business, I set about a bigger goal—well, stock availability of course, and particularly with one supplier. I visited their factory, learnt all about them, and started to work closely with their teams. After several months of hard graft and following the Six Sigma framework of **DMAIC** (**Define, Measure, Analyse, Improve, and Control**), the project was complete. I now had to get the finance team to agree to the annualised savings I was claiming using data I had started to collate and some forward forecasting. I was then to get the final sign off for my project. I was absolutely delighted when the team came back and agreed that my project would save the business approximately **£100,000 per year**. I sent all of the documents off and was over the moon to be awarded my **Lean Six Sigma Green Belt**. This has gone on to help me with so many projects. The amount I learnt from this experience was fantastic. I have this absolute love for learning now. ***Why was it so different to my experience at school?***

I was offered a place on a prestigious Management Development Program that would be run over the next six months. I was to go to lots of classroom-based events and do the **Insights** course again. I knew what to expect this time. We went through our reports in the classroom, but there were no surprises. My green colour had increased, meaning my people skills had improved a little, but not much change. It described me as **'a strategic thinker who can clearly see the flaws and benefits of most situations. It said that I took great pleasure from maximizing efficiency and cost effectiveness and that I could grasp complex concepts and find creative solutions to problems. It described me as calm and quiet, an analytical thinker that shows little emotional response to situations outwardly and can, if involved in conflict situations such as criticism, withdraw into himself.'** This was just all spot on. How could they be so accurate with just 50 questions? I was embarrassed by as much of this as I was impressed. I wanted to be better, I wanted to be more.

One moment that really shone out for me was an exercise about story telling. We watched an excerpt of a **TEDeX** talk about Dame Gillian Lynn. She was seen as a trouble maker at school and disruptive. The speaker said how her Mum had taken her to the Doctors. She was fidgety and couldn't sit still. The speaker stated that had it been nowadays, she would have been diagnosed with **ADHD** and given medication, but that ADHD wasn't something you could have back then. The Doctor suggested that Gillian wasn't naughty, but in fact a dancer, and that her Mum should take her to a dance school. She did just that and Gillian excelled there and ended up becoming a multi-millionaire and the choreographer of *Cats the Musical*! This would stay with me for years and I still think about it now, it had such an impact. Not for the way the story was told, but the story itself.

It was on this course that I also found out about some amazing books. It was here that I learnt about **emotional intelligence**. A life-changing book was ***How To Win Friends and Influence People*** by Dale Carnegie. In Dale's book there is a quote that reads, **'The greatest discovery of my generation is that a human being can alter his life by altering his attitudes.'** I wanted to alter my life. I desperately wanted to alter my life. It had a real impact, and I learnt so much from that book. I had a thirst for knowledge, and other books I read after this included, ***7 Habits of Highly Effective People* by Stephen Covey**, ***Who Moved My Cheese***, ***Fish***, along with anything I could absorb about **emotional intelligence**.

We learnt about change and how people don't like change. We learnt how to communicate effectively, how to deal with conflict and so much more. We practised situations with role plays and learnt in many different interactive ways.

The course was amazing, and at the end we had to present a project. I remember this well, a room with the teaching staff and a group of regional managers and directors. As I spoke I could literally feel my knee caps shaking, I was just hoping they couldn't see it. Then, back in the classroom, we had to give each other feedback. We would write on post-it notes and go and put them on a board under the person's name they applied to. I still have those exact post-it notes **11 years on**.

They read as follows:

- Gavin, very knowledgeable, thanks for all the info.
- Great support to the team, amazing mate.
- Enormous potential, **WILL BE AT THE TOP.**
- Gavin, don't fold on your opinion.
- Fountain of knowledge!!
- Gav, you have great knowledge + passion - don't forget to go for a result - I'm sure you do :-)
- Gavin - some great ideas over the last couple of days. Great advice on other's projects.

I was made up. I was so pleased with these, and I often look at them, especially on days I feel down or like I'm not good enough. However, at the time I didn't truly believe them, I just thought they were just saying it or being sarcastic, especially the one about being at the top. Now, 11 years later, I do have much more belief and can almost accept it. Honestly, I really am my own worst critic.

Back to the office, and with two great projects in the bag—one for the team and one for my Lean Six Sigma project—we continued the push. We were such a great team, and got on so well. I did kind of embarrass myself once though. I was talking over the desk to one of the team who had been delivering the game. I looked up to her, totally innocent, and said, **"Are you going on the game tomorrow?"** It didn't cross my mind that this had a dual meaning. She burst out laughing. It took me a second to click. *Oh no, I had just insinuated she was a prostitute!* She knew what I meant though. We all just got each other, and it was laughs like that we had then that made us become closer. I'm still in contact with that lovely lady today.

The Data Obsession

I started to get much more into data in the business. We had just started to use something new to me that was called a data lake. It was a place where billions of rows and columns of data would be stored in tables. There was a programming language called SQL that you could write that enabled you to query this data, to ask it questions. You could also join these data tables if they had a matching column such as the date and make bigger tables with even more detailed information and add calculated columns. The possibilities were endless. You could then create visualisations and bring those millions of rows of data to life with simple graphs and charts. I loved it. It was time for another book. I bought a book called ***An Introduction To SQL***, a mammoth of a book at over **1,000 pages**. I was amounting a few books on my desk by this point, and one manager asked me if I had actually read them. **"Of course,"** I said. I was building tables, analysing data, and giving people real deep insights into the business and the stock we had. I'd build dashboards. These were multiple visualisations like graphs all on one screen looking at millions of rows of data. You could then click on a bar on a chart for example to get another chart in the next layer of detail down. In fact, how I built them, you could keep on clicking and drilling down from the company's total sales on screws to a particular single purchase of a box of screws and see how much profit it made, who sold it, what shelf it was on the branch and who the customer was. You could then enact that information to improve the business. I absolutely loved this and grew a real passion for it. Once word got out, I would have people approach me to build dashboards for them, for their area of the business. I said to people it was easy and gave them instructions on how, but they still came back to me. My assumption then was these people were just being lazy as it was so easy. I loved helping though and I was so passionate about the business so I just did it, I just loved helping people and couldn't say no.

The next thing to start tackling was dead stock, and there was another business in the group that had a team of five people all looking at stock across the network that wasn't selling in that area, but was selling in another area of the business. By bringing this back to base on an empty delivery truck, we could redistribute it and save on purchasing fresh stock. It was a bit like what I was doing back at the branch in distributing the stock out, but on a massive scale. I knew the benefit of this was to keep cash in the business from my accountancy training, and from my Lean Six Sigma training I recognised the waste of inventory sat there gathering dust: the waste of it having to be counted again and again, and the waste of the trucks coming back to the warehouse empty all but for some pallets. I travelled over and saw what they were doing. I got it. It was pretty simple really. Find what stock was not selling in one area that was selling in another, ensure that they had over the minimum quantity so as to not trigger another order, then arrange for the branch to put it on a pallet. Finally, then arrange for the delivery truck to take it back to the warehouse where other branches could order it. It would save thousands, especially on stock from far away places like China where you had to buy a container load at a time.

I drove home that day deep in thought. From what I knew about data and spreadsheets, I could even take waste away from this process. I got to work. The next day I excitedly arranged for myself to get use of a programme called **Microsoft Access**. It was a database that could sort and store millions of lines of data. I also bought yet another book, this time on **VBA code**, a programming language you could use in an **Excel** spreadsheet that created an automation known as a **macro** (basically the programming did some of the work for you). With a computer system called **SAP Business Objects, Access, Excel, VBA code, and a copy of the form the other branch was using**, I got to work. A few weeks later, I cracked it. I created a system that would search for slow and dead moving stock in branches that were selling elsewhere that we stocked in the warehouse with quantities greater than the required minimum to be held in a branch. With a press of a button, the coding would search and find what we needed and create nearly 600 forms, one for each branch, telling the manager what we needed, what quantity, and when it would be picked up. Then it would also create the collection schedule and send it to the distribution team. **It worked like a dream; it did the work of those five people.** I then used my analytics and newly found IT skills to create a dashboard. This was a one-page view of the value of goods brought back to base and the savings it had generated. By the time I left the business around six years later, the process was still going and had saved the business over **£11 million** plus the wages of five people over all of those years! **This is without doubt one of my proudest ever achievements.**

With this now in the bag, I was wanting to finish my last exam for the Management Accounting qualification from **CIMA**, and I could use the letters **CIMA Cert BA** after my name. Wow, this meant so much to me. I approached the management and was asked to write a business case for the company to fund it. To my delight, they did. I booked a course right away and got started.

Chapter 14 - The A Word

The Stigma and the Scapegoat

It was now **2018**. Oliver was almost **seven** and in primary school, and things weren't going well. For some time now, we were in constant contact with the school: "*Oliver did this.*" "*Oliver did that.*"

Oliver was so quiet though and so loving, but we knew there were problems. Just taking him out to the park some days caused horrific problems. He'd kick and fight and scream. He hated going to school; he'd try to run away. He'd hide under tables in class with his hands on his ears. Oliver's learning was getting behind, and his social skills were not good. On school sports day one year, it was heartbreaking seeing him struggle on balancing beams and catching things; he still just couldn't do it. When he played up at home, the guidance from family was to give him a good whack and bring him in line. Apparently this worked once for a family member when he kicked off and didn't want to go in a shop; this was how you dealt with kids like this. From then on, we really didn't want to leave him with family.

We were told about **Autism** and that we should look into getting Oliver diagnosed. I had blamed anything out of the ordinary on **Chicken Pox** up until now. My story was that it must have done something to his neurological pathways while he was developing in the womb; this is what I would tell everyone. I couldn't comprehend that it was Autism. After all, I knew about Autism: it meant you couldn't talk, it meant you might have learning difficulties or that you were like the characters from films like *Rain Man* or *Mercury Rising*. **In fact, just 40 years prior, in the 80's, children with Autism would be in mental asylums chained to radiators and given electric shock therapy.** Oliver was nothing like this. Besides, school and family were probably more correct: it needed better parenting. **WE** were the problem.

But this had started long ago. I even remember one journey back from a holiday in Cornwall, when Oliver was much younger. Oliver screamed all the way home. We tried everything we could think of but were travelling down the motorway. He just wouldn't stop. It was horrendous. We pulled over in the services to change him, feed him, etc., but we just couldn't stop him. We could not work out the reason. We had tried everything. People just stared at us like we were useless, and we felt it too.

The Mirror

We continued on, constantly getting emails and calls from the school. We were now really starting to struggle. What was happening? We once again had **Autism** brought up, so I decided to do some research. Wow, Autism was nothing like I thought. In fact, I learnt about **ADHD** too; I just went with what everyone else around me said about it before this. It was poor parenting and out-of-control kids, people giving their kids Red Bull and going to the doctors just to claim benefits—it was all over social media which was big by now. **I feel so ashamed of those thoughts now.** In fact, what I was learning about Autism described Oliver exactly. I thought he might be Autistic, but this was embarrassing. How could I tell people my kid was Autistic? The shame. I really wanted to continue to blame the Chicken Pox.

We needed answers, though, and we needed support, and I kept on researching. The more I learnt, the more it described not just Oliver, but **ME**. ***How can this be? Nah, if I was Autistic someone would have picked it up by the time I was 40! Surely?*** I did an online test. I knew it wasn't official, but I was too embarrassed to go for a proper test. The result said it was highly likely that I was at the higher end of the Autistic Spectrum and had something called **Asperger's**. I had heard of this before; my sister, who I didn't really have much contact with at this point, had a daughter with Asperger's. Apparently, it described someone that had higher intelligence. Well, this didn't count in my case; I wasn't exactly the most intelligent. Someone that struggles with social interaction. *Yes, yes, that is definitely me*. And someone that had intense interest in things to the point of obsession—that was definitely me. It went on that they might be good at spotting patterns, be good at numbers, but might struggle with social cues, body language, and sarcasm, and were susceptible to having anxiety and depression. It explained me to a tee, but, *I'm 40, I* *struggled massively at school and went to the Doctors countless times and no one said I was Autistic or had Asperger's.* I asked Paul to do the same test and Kerry and others too. No, normal. *What? What the hell is going on here?* I wanted to believe it, but I couldn't be. I didn't really want to be Autistic. Besides, people who are Autistic are disabled. I'm not disabled. I have worked all my life and have a good job. Please excuse my ignorance at this point; it was all the thoughts I was brought up with: misinformation and lack of education. I then thought back to my **Insights** profile. That had now been done twice, both with almost exact results. It basically described someone with Asperger's. It all started to piece together.

I was later to learn that **Asperger's** would stop being used as a diagnosis. This was due to a link between Hans Asperger, who named the condition after himself, and the **Nazis**. Hans Asperger described many of these children as being less worthwhile, and many were sent to be killed during the Holocaust in World War II. There is now no separate diagnosis of Asperger's; it is all encompassed in the diagnosis of **Autism Spectrum Disorder (ASD)**. Many people still use the term Asperger's for their own diagnosis due to the stigma around Autism. That's how bad it has been.

The Mid-Life Crisis and the Genius

Oliver started on the path to an official diagnosis. It was a battle that would go on for over four years and even go to mediation to get him the support he needed. School just saw him as naughty. The family just said he needed a good whack. Experts said he was just wired differently. We were mentally torn apart.

I was still trying to push on with my career and, due to the project I ran for dead stock and my Lean Six Sigma Project, I was asked by the Supply Chain Director if I would go on something called a secondment. It was a temporary step up, with a pay rise, working as **Stock and Systems Manager** at the **UK Distribution Centre**. I would have two direct reports and a total team of 23 people across two shifts and be responsible for all of the stock and the systems for a warehouse the size of two and a half football pitches. There were over **80** articulated trucks in and out every day, over **98,000** different product codes, and nearly **350** staff. It was a monster. The stock audit at the end of the year for the last few years hadn't been great. One of my tasks was to sort this.

I got to work and would go to different sites and meetings. One thing that ashamed me though was my tatty old Mondeo; everyone I dealt with in Management had lovely cars. In fact, on the way home to fill up with petrol after work one day, I went to pay for fuel and one of Kerry's relatives was working at the till. I didn't know she worked there. She asked why I drove an old banger of a car but Kerry had a brand new one. I told her that my family was more important than me and that Kerry did the school run and that was why. I just saved my money instead. She mentioned that I should save my money and gave me a reason why—it was deeply offensive and related to our children, something I cannot repeat in this book, but something I knew had absolutely no truth. It caused a huge family argument. It turns out that it was a ploy, a ploy of pure jealousy. Kerry's relative had mentioned to another relative that she wanted to split us up so Kerry would end up in a council house again just like she was. As we moved up the social ladder, this jealousy would appear more and more, but Kerry and I are a team, inseparable, and stuff like that just moved us closer together.

I was a bit down about my car though and felt inferior to others when I went to meetings. I was turning forty and had heard all the stories about men having a mid-life crisis and buying a sportscar. **So I did just that.** Kerry and I went out on my birthday looking for a car I would be proud to drive. I was a car fanatic anyway. A few weeks later, I ended up buying a used **Porsche Boxster Turbo S** in gloss black. It was immaculate, had an electric convertible roof, electric rear spoiler, lush leather interior, huge alloy wheels, and was incredibly fast. I would drive it and just smile ear to ear, looking in the side mirror at the glorious curves of the rear wing. I also got a personalised number plate with **GAV** on it. However, it used a lot of fuel, and one day I had to pull back into that petrol station. I saw Kerry's relative on the till from the forecourt. I didn't like to boast, but what she had tried was pure evil. I walked into the shop, smiled at her and said, **"Oh, I got rid of the old banger, I've got a Porsche now, a private plate too."** She never said a word. I'm not a guy that takes revenge, but that was so damn satisfying. My Mum found out I had a Porsche too. It wasn't massively expensive compared to some. I got a message from her:

"Hi, I heard you have a Porsche now. How on earth did you afford that?" No pride, just pure jealousy.

In January of 2018, I went to work, analysing data and designing processes. I worked my socks off. During this time, a new Manager came in. I wanted to impress. We had a meeting as an official introduction to each other. I just wanted to show what I could do and be noticed, and I shared with him a one-page document showing what I had achieved so far and what my goals were. He looked at it briefly, gave it back to me and said, **"Well, if you read that, you would think you were the saint of [company name redacted]. You need to sort this place out."** My heart sank. I felt emotional. It was like he had just punched me in the stomach. I felt sick. I carried on though, but it really affected me.

There was something that happened during this role that will stay with me for the rest of my life that I would like to share with you. There was a guy, in his 50s, that worked on the night shift counting stock. He was known as being a weirdo and militant. He looked different. He had grey hair in a long pony tail, was on the larger side, and was always unshaven. He often wore prog rock T-shirts like Led Zeppelin or Pink Floyd, and he liked to speak his mind. For the purpose of the book I will call him Ivan. Ivan had come up with some coding to create a programme to get information from the stock system to help us. It was way more technical than I could have done, and it would have cost us hundreds of thousands to have that developed by a software company. What was more impressive was that I found out that Ivan was a carer for his disabled wife during the day when he wasn't sleeping, but had still managed to write this code in his spare time. To me, he was a **genius**. I was so impressed and so intrigued that I went in to work at midnight one night to personally hand him an award. We called it a **'Getting It Right'** award, and it came with a gift voucher. Ivan wouldn't shake my hand. He stated he didn't like germs. You could see others snigger. Had this been nowadays after **COVID**, you might understand it, but this was before that had ever been around. It didn't bother me though. Ivan was delighted with the award. You could see it meant a lot to him, and to be honest, it meant a lot to me that I could do that for him. I talked to him for a while about what he had done and he told me of his dream to become a computer programmer. It was a second language to him, but he didn't do well at school, and so this was his only option. I was so impressed and felt sorry for Ivan. I knew what that felt like. I contacted IT and spoke to management, but no one was interested in a fifty-year-old warehouse worker that spoke his mind. I knew why Ivan spoke his mind though: he cared. He cared a lot, and he wanted things right. He knew when things could be done better, and to him it just caused sheer frustration.

When I left this role, I stayed in touch with Ivan and we would email each other occasionally. One week I emailed Ivan but he didn't reply back straight away like he usually did. Eventually, a couple of weeks later I got an email. **"Hi, I'm sorry I didn't reply back straight away. I've been in the hospital. I have cancer and it's bad. They have given me just a few weeks left to live."** I was heartbroken. Poor Ivan, he had so much talent. His genius was wasted. I felt so bad as I could see his brilliance but no one else could. I still think about Ivan a lot and **his story powers me to make a difference. Every time I think about just shutting up and cracking on, I remember Ivan. I have to tell my story. I have to share Ivan's story. I have to make a difference in his memory.**

The Final Collapse

I was now getting near to taking my final exam in the certificate level and got it booked. Nervously, I sat it. I passed, but with just a small margin. I was so excited, so happy though, just to get through. I went to get my phone to call Kerry and dropped it and smashed the screen. It was only a week or two old. For a second I was gutted, but not for long because this ex-binman, this useless failure, was now becoming an accountant!

Feeling so proud and on top of the world, I thought I would let my mum know. We didn't speak much, but surely she would be proud of this. I just had to tell her. **"Mum, I passed my final certificate exam. I'm so happy. I have the letters CIMA Cert BA after my name now, something I never thought I'd achieve,"** I said. The reply wasn't as good as I expected: **"Oh that's good, love. Your sister has letters after her name; she did an online dog grooming course."** I felt deflated, again, just nothing there at all, not the slightest bit of pride. I had worked so hard for this. I had put in hundreds if not thousands of hours and pushed myself so hard, but my achievements were compared to an online dog grooming course. It made me sad. I wondered why I had even bothered calling her.

Back at work, the culture there grew ever more toxic in the office. I just felt out of place. There was another manager put in between myself and this new manager. He was worse, absolutely brutal. Staff were leaving and more coming in. I started to struggle, but I really wanted to deliver. In a meeting one day, with **HR** present, I was pointed at and told, **"If this audit goes wrong, the bullets are for you."** I sat there quiet, petrified. No one said a thing. They just carried on like it was a normal thing to say. I'd been in meetings with the Supply Chain Director and had been given strict instructions on what to say and what not to say by my manager. Half of what was being said wasn't true, and this manager was getting a pat on the back for it. It really got to me, I felt a huge sense of injustice. He would tell me not to speak to certain Directors and tell me not to share solutions to problems with them. I started to really go down hill with my mental health. Then the brain fog started again. I could feel myself going back into a burnout. ***Not again*, what the hell was wrong with me?**

I tried to speak to the Supply Chain Director. He told me, **"I think you think you are better than you are."** It hit me. *Yes, maybe he was right*. This was a stretch too far. I was just lucky. My teachers, parents, and some of my managers before were right. **I was useless. I was ashamed, why did I even bother.**

I had two people that supported me at that time: a lovely young lady I'll call Jennifer. Jennifer was head of finance—we had some great chats about future goals and she said I should continue my CIMA studies and get into Finance—I was apprehensive though, the finance team had all been to university, they were different to me. The other was a fantastic guy I'll call Mark. He was there as a consultant helping us look at automation and bringing two warehouses together into one. Without these two I'd have struggled even more; they were the only two people I could talk to. I had talked to Mark about my aspirations to also become a consultant one day. I loved projects and business improvement. Mark and I are still in contact today.

One day, I just desperately wanted to be with my son for school sports day. I knew he would struggle. I had to be there for him, so I arranged with my team that I would be out that morning. After all, I had worked way more than my hours of late and being salaried, with no extra pay, and I knew I was paid a huge amount less than my predecessor. I am glad I went. He struggled, just like he always did. He just couldn't do what the others could do and they kept trying again and again to get him to do it. He tried to run away. I was so sad.

I was now in a really low place: my son was struggling, work was toxic, and I couldn't stop thinking about the fact that I might also be **Autistic**. I was a bit of a mess. I headed back to work. I walked past the manager's office. **"Where the fuck have you been?"**

"I've been at my son's school sports day to support him," I replied.

"What? What do you mean? There's fucking work to do here!" I lost it. I hated conflict. I broke down in tears. It was like my mind was a watering can. The issues I was having were filling it up and up, and this was a drop too much; it just overflowed. The manager looked shocked and said, **"I think you better take yourself home."**

I was broken again. **Why did this keep happening to me? Why, why, why?** I knew why: **I was useless**. I was a waste of space. I couldn't handle pressure. Those post-it notes, yes they were just mocking me. I was a laughing stock. Why do I even bother? I drove home not actually wanting to go home. I just wanted to drive off a bridge into a river that day. I was a failure, a disgrace to my kids and Kerry. Again, here I was, useless me, struggling to cope. I couldn't though, I couldn't leave the kids with no Dad. I couldn't leave Kerry on her own. I had to somehow get through this.

The Final Word

I went to the Doctors. Again, I felt like I just wanted the world to stop for a bit so I could get off. I had had this feeling before. I needed a break. I felt like I was trapped inside my body again looking out again, that feeling that I was just watching a movie as myself but not actually there. I got through the brain fog to the doctors office and I broke down. I was already on anti-depressants. I mentioned **Autism**. The Doctor ruled it out. He said, **"Even if you are Autistic, you've got this far. What's a diagnosis going to do for you? You just need some rest and some CBT."** I'd had that before, but it didn't work for long. I'd be fine for ages, and then I would just get someone that would make me feel like absolute shit and it would all fall apart. I couldn't carry on like this.

I was signed off with a breakdown related to stress for six weeks. I couldn't see anyone. I didn't even want to leave the house. I could hardly function. I was a mess. A few weeks passed, and Mark messaged me asking if I would like to meet for coffee. I was apprehensive. I didn't really want to leave the house. I had massive social anxiety. He was amazing though and seemed to just get it. I eventually decided I would go. I felt sick with anxiety and just didn't want to be there, but I knew I had to get better. Mark was amazing. He just listened. He didn't judge. He was just there. I will never forget that. **He possibly saved my life.** I really was in a dark place

Chapter 15 - A Revelation

The Discovery of Meditation

While I was resting, I saw an advert for a beginners' meditation class at a local **Buddhist Centre**. I knew the place from our weekend bike riding with the running club; they had the most amazing cafe and it made an excellent cake stop. To me, though, it was all a bit hippy and **joss sticks** and too religious—again, just an uneducated mind. I heard that meditation was good though, so as I was in such a dark place, I thought I would give it a try. I couldn't go alone though; I was too nervous. We arranged a babysitter and Kerry joined me.

It was so different from what I thought. I loved how quiet it was. I felt relaxed and welcome. I learnt that meditation wasn't religious at all, or didn't have to be. I also learnt that you didn't sit with your legs crossed humming with flowers behind your ears. The meditation teacher taking our session actually used to work in an office in London in a highly paid corporate job. She got fed up with the hustle and bustle, found Buddhism, and became a member of the Buddhist Community—I could relate to that.

We started off breathing deeply and blowing out as hard as we could. We then had to shut our eyes and relax and just concentrate on the breath right at the end of our noses, just hone in on that. I tried, but my mind wandered. The teacher told us that we will get thoughts as we do this, but think of them as bubbles, allow them to appear but bring yourself back to that breath and allow those bubbles to just fade away and pop. Actually, this was working. Next up, we did an exercise where we would keep our eyes closed, imagine a bright white smoke full of goodness, happiness, and joy, and breathe it in deeply through your nose. Okay, it was going a bit hippy, but I went along with it. Next, we were to blow out as hard as we could until no breath remained, and this time, we were to imagine a thick black intoxicating smoke full of our stress, our worries, and all of our negativity. It was amazing; I came home feeling the best I had felt in ages. This was it. I worked at it and worked at it, and felt better and better.

Running from the Black Dog

To help with recovery, I continued my running and cycling. I found that it helped me so much; it was probably one of the biggest aids of my recovery. I would hit the trails and just run and run and run. By now, I was running marathons and had even completed a **100-mile cycle ride**. I found it so helpful in my recovery that I decided to write a blog called '**Running From The Black Dog'**. I also set up a Facebook Group to help others start to run for the benefit of their mental health. The Facebook group is still running today.

I now needed to return to work. I really didn't want to go back. The thought of working in that environment again filled me with dread. I was invited for a meeting with the Supply Chain Director. I was nervous and felt like a failure, but I remembered my breathing and used it walking through the car park. I was expecting the worst. *I was a failure, useless. I had let everyone down again.* He was actually understanding. We spoke about medication and how I felt. He got it. He gave me some advice: **"Do as I did. Go and find the root cause, find what's driving it."** That stuck with me. He told me that the audit had passed for the first time. It was the first time in three years this had happened. **It was a success;** that made me happy. He also said that I didn't have to go back there, **ever**, and that I could start, when I was ready, and only when I was ready, back in my old job and I could keep the same money. I was taken aback; I couldn't believe it. This was amazing; it had been on my mind so much. It was a huge relief.

The Finance Analyst

Early **2019**, and I headed back to the office, on strict instructions to take it easy. I had a new manager and he was really understanding and showed genuine concern. I worked with some of the old team, a couple of new ones, and we pushed on with stock availability, this time mainly around timber. Within a few weeks, I was fully back on my feet and chomping at the bit for more, and in the next seven months, we smashed it.

There was however, another embarrassing moment. There's a pattern building, isn't there! One day, someone came rushing out of the corridor where the toilets were saying someone had collapsed. I was a First Aider and the nearest one there. I rushed to their aid. There was this lady I knew who sat a few desks away from me just in a bundle on the floor where she had dropped, I knew she had issues with low blood pressure, my training kicked in. I looked for danger, checked for vital signs and shouted for someone to call an ambulance. I then shook their shoulders looking for a response. **"Claire, Claire, can you hear me?"** Nothing, but she was breathing and had a pulse. I put her in the recovery position, well it was near enough, I never did master it, and continued to call her name to try and wake her. **"Claire, Claire, can you hear me?"** Suddenly she came around. "**It's Kerry!**" Her name was **Kerry,** how could I get it so wrong, especially when my wife's name is Kerry. What an absolute idiot! I was so embarrassed but Kerry was fine, just a little dazed. We would laugh about this incident for years to come. I have never been good with facial recognition, even watching TV I would get characters confused and have to ask Kerry who was who. Walking around the office I would try and look at peoples name badges to remember their name, unless of course there was something that really made them stand out. I was later to find that this was yet another Autistic trait.

I was then asked to interview for a project role working on supply chain development. It would be reporting up to Jennifer. I interviewed, did some tests, and got the job! We spoke often. She was, and still is, an amazing **leader**, and it was at this time that I realised there was a difference between a manager and a leader. I spoke with Jennifer about my desire to prove myself and how I wanted to become an accountant, but how I was also so worried as I hadn't been to university like everyone else and had lived a very different life. Jennifer reassured me that I didn't need qualifications, I was good at my job and had proved myself, but that there was always a chance there. I wanted it badly, but I was also hesitant. I just didn't feel enough, and to be honest, not feeling enough was possibly why I wanted a qualification. I needed to really prove, not just to others, but to myself, that I wasn't useless and I had as much right to work in the corporate world as anyone else, whatever my background or educational experience.

Taking the job on, I worked for a Manager that had also worked up from the shop floor and had completed a qualification later in life; in fact, it was a **Master's in Supply Chain**. We got along with each other and worked so well together. We often travelled the country and delivered projects. That role was to be fairly short lived though, at just another seven months in tenure; the project team would then be disbanded.

Meanwhile, running and cycling was becoming even more of an obsession. I loved it. In fact, it was time to step it up a notch; I wanted to run an **ultra marathon**. An ultra marathon is anything over 26.2 miles, with 26.2 miles being a marathon. Many people around me were running them, and I just loved pushing myself further and further. Some of the guys were doing 100-mile ultras. I never could do that, but I really wanted to go further, I loved pushing myself. I got a buzz out of doing something I once thought I couldn't. I did it with everything, always pushing outside of my comfort zone. Even speaking in front of people and presenting started to become easier. I found that with anything, the more I pushed through that awkward feeling the easier it got, then I would push some more.

In June 2019, I took on an ultra marathon called **Shire and Spires**, a **35-mile timed run** through the rolling countryside of Northamptonshire. I ran with a group of others from the club; we were there to support each other. The day was roasting hot, way too hot for running really, but this was it; we had trained for months for this. It was going so well. We completed the half marathon marker at 13.1 miles, and on we went. We walked the hills and ran the flats and downhills—that was our plan to get around, especially in that heat. By just over 20 miles I was starting to lag. I told the others to crack on, and I would slow it down a bit. I really started to struggle by mile 25 as we hit an old disused railway track, a monotonous straight run on a gravel path, the sun beating down on us. I was drinking as much as I could, but just sweating it straight back out. At **27.66 miles** we had just gone through a gate into a field, and that was it. I was done. I had a huge pain in my kidneys and just dropped to the floor; I couldn't run another step. Luckily, one of the guys had stayed with me. He panicked a bit as I dropped down and quickly got a spare water bottle out of his backpack and poured it over my head. It was heaven! **"You went a bit white then, mate, you OK?"**

"Yeah I'm fine, you crack on, you're nearly there, keep going, I'll get back."

"Not a chance," he said, **"your run is over, you're not going anywhere and neither am I."** He had given up his race for me; I felt so damn guilty. He called the support vehicle, or **the bus of shame** as I called it, and we headed back to race HQ. I was gutted I had failed. All I could do now was to get to the finish line to cheer my other friends over the line. One day, **I will run that race again, and I'll complete it. I'm adamant about that.**

It was that summer that **Jennifer** approached me again. **"I have a new role I'm recruiting for in Finance. I'd like you to apply, I think you'd be great."** The role was as a **Finance Analyst** for **Digital and Supply Chain**, an area I knew a lot about. I was excited but hesitant. This was it. I would be working across at the finance end of the office with all the intelligent people that had university degrees and spoke posher than me. I so wanted to do this. It was my dream and had been for a few years. This was reality; I was actually about to become a real accountant. I was so worried as to not make myself look stupid though. I thought long and hard and I emailed **Jennifer**. I could see her down at the finance end of the office, but I was too nervous to go and speak to her. I popped her an email, **"Jennifer, I have thought about it. I'm going to go for it."** I looked over, and **Jennifer** walked towards me, a huge beaming smile on her face. **"I am so happy, you will HAVE to study and get your qualification now,"** she said. **"You are going to be great."**

"I hope so," I said. **"I don't want to let you down."**

I just couldn't wait to tell Kerry. I was so excited: this was it. From that dream when I was in a dark place, a thought that once seemed an impossibility, I was here. I was about to become a proper accountant, albeit one that had a lot to learn. Kerry was so proud, and as soon as I walked through the door, she gave me a massive hug. **"I told you you could do it, I have always believed in you."**

I started in January **2020**. It was hard at first; people were talking a language I didn't really know apart from some courses and exams I had taken. I felt like a massive fake, but this was my chance and I wasn't going to throw it away. I was to report in to that most amazing person, for the book I'll call her Sam. She was probably the best manager I have ever had. I knew she had my back and I knew she genuinely cared. This, I had found, was a rare quality! It made me relax though. I was way out of my comfort zone and so worried about making a mistake, but Sam just had this way that would help me remain calm even when things were hard. Things were so good that I went to the doctor and arranged to come off anti-depressants. Life was great despite being in a whole new world. It turns out, these people in finance were just like me. I just seemed to get along with them better than anywhere I had ever worked. **I had found my tribe.** It was also so great to be around such a mix of people from all sorts of backgrounds, and I learnt so much about different cultures. It really started to expand my mind. I have to say, I was so lucky to have a Manager like Sam, because what was to happen next totally threw my life upside down, but would also then become one of the best things that happened to me.

Chapter 16 - COVID

The Remote Chaos

March 23rd, 2020: the first COVID lockdown! In an instant, we were all sent home—I believe it was actually a day or two before this. There I was, new in finance, learning the ropes, and I was suddenly thrust into a world of working from a wobbly camping table in the corner of a room at home with the stress of kids not at school and not wanting to do school work at home. **IT WAS HELL!** What made it worse, I was a stress eater, and there were Easter eggs still left over from Easter all around; I binged to get me through. I also stopped running apart from on the home treadmill. The running group still continued despite government rules, but I just couldn't break the rules. My anxiety about getting COVID went through the roof, and I became sedentary. It didn't help that I was about to also embark on thousands of hours of study for my professional qualification. I have to say, if it wasn't for Sam, I probably would have given up. Sam was so supportive and certainly went above and beyond. There were some wobbles, but with the meditation, Kerry and I being there for each other, and a most amazing manager, we got through.

Once everything started to settle a bit I started to realise that, actually, how amazing it was to work from home. There was no sitting in traffic every morning and I could spend more time with my family. I could also work uninterrupted once the kids were back at school. I could really hyperfocus. It brought me back to being in the school office, no one to disturb me and I could get lost in my work, I began to love it. I even started to see a change in my energy levels and productivity.

During the next year and a bit in this role, I started to actually be able to do some work that related to my studies too. As I was studying, it was fantastic and really helped me to bring it to life and understand it. I also used my love of improving processes and cutting out waste. I built a complete purchase order system from scratch, which enabled better reporting and control of spending. This was trialled in the main UK distribution centre and then eventually rolled out to the rest of the supply chain. The best thing of all was that I built it all from learning another computer coding language called AppScript, and therefore it cost nothing to implement, apart from my time. I rebuilt every accounting process from top to bottom, automating it to cut down non-value-added work, allowing me more time to help improve the business, and reduced the costs of manual handling equipment by tracking usage for the first time and thus reducing the fleet we hired. I was in my element again and producing outstanding work over and above my remit. Yet I still doubted myself. I still had that **imposter syndrome** and felt a lot less than anyone else. I just wanted to prove I was worthy, yet I still had the voices of my teachers and parents and ex bosses running through my head telling me I was useless. Please, never do that to a child, it **NEVER** leaves them.

Social Media Attack

Part of what really helped me feel good was writing my **Running From The Black Dog** blog. It really did help me, and I loved it that I was helping others. It had now become quite popular, and I had a big following. I had decided I would get a local business to print some running t-shirts with the logo on and sell them, with the profit going to a mental health charity, **The Mental Health Foundation**. They were really popular, and I raised a fair bit of money for the charity. It really made me feel good that I was giving back.

I advertised them on my **LinkedIn** page, and one of the runners from the local club made a horrific comment on it, slating me that I was just doing this for the likes and I shouldn't be promoting myself on LinkedIn and that no one wanted to hear about mental health. He was really harsh; it hit me like a tonne of bricks. It continued over into Facebook. He was on a mission to bring me down, and the club had become elitist and cliquey.

Thinking back now, yes, there was an element of me that did it for the likes. I had always wanted to be liked. I always felt alone, even in a room full of people. It was so great that I could help others, raise money for charity, but also get some recognition. I felt sick. I hated conflict. I just couldn't carry on with it. I just thought, *I have other battles to fight. I just can't do this.* I deleted my Facebook account and Instagram. That was it; social media was over for me. I had to focus. I had to give my energy to my studies and my family. There was only so much I could give. I regret it now, I really do. The Facebook group is still going though, and I have since opened a new Facebook account, but I have no friends on it and use it very differently. The Facebook page with my blog is still live today along with a chat group. I eventually gave up running too; the buzz was gone. I just saw the club as a place of negativity but dearly missed many of the members.

It was then that I decided I needed to change the way I dealt with what others thought and said about me as it was really affecting me. I added another book to my collection, **'The Courage To Be Disliked'** by Fumitake Koga and Ichiro Kishimi. This fascinating book helped me to reframe my thinking somewhat. It taught me about getting freedom from my past, in my case, all of those people that had told me I was useless. I had to change the way I thought. I had to use the meditation example of the bubbles popping every time I thought about the past. The book mentioned it was not my task to decide if someone liked me or disliked me and therefore I should not try to control it, that I could not control their decision. I had to start to see others as equal to me and not far superior and, above all, I had to have the courage to be disliked and the courage to be my true authentic self.

The EHCP Fight and the Second Diagnosis

It was still hard with Oliver, and we were battling to get a diagnosis for him in order to allow him to get the support he needed. It took up so much time, and it was so hard to get information. Every county did things differently. There was no one point of call. Their system was a nightmare. You could hardly get to talk to anyone. In **July 2020**, we had been refused help, and we then took the process to mediation. We had to get this sorted. The aim was to get Oliver an **EHCP (Education and Health Care Plan)**. This would last him until he was 21 and enable the school to get funding to help him to get the help he needed. Such stressful times and all whilst trying to study and work full time, but I wasn't giving up on any of it.

With all of the pressure, it was a struggle, but having such a great manager was helping to hold my head above water. I wanted to grow stronger though. I wanted to develop personally and become more resilient. There is no way I wanted to end up with another burnout, not now I was starting to realise my dream of becoming an accountant. I felt I had to go back to the doctor. I knew that previously I was told to just crack on as I had hit 40 and that a diagnosis wouldn't make any difference, but I just had to know.

I went back and saw a different doctor. He got it. He understood and agreed that it would be helpful for me. He referred me. It was such a huge relief; finally someone was listening to me. Finally I was on the route to getting some answers. I was added to the waiting list and was told it would take around **three years!**

I started working on self improvement a lot as well as working and studying as I was adamant I wasn't going to crash and burn this time. I was still on a mission to make myself stronger and I also wanted to be a voice for Oliver and make a difference to him and all other **Autistic** children.

The Neurodiversity Mandate

I had found, through my research, that the term **neurodiversity** was first used by an Australian Sociologist called Judy Singer in the 1990s; Judy is **Neurodivergent** herself, being on the Autistic Spectrum. **Neurodiversity** is a term used to describe the human population. Every one of us is different and unique, made up of how our brains are wired and the journey and experiences we have had in life. **Neurotypical** however is a brain that is the most common denominator and is the brain type that everything in society is aligned to and in fact, what the education system is based on. **Neurodivergent** is a brain that is wired differently from the neurotypical person.

While all of this was going on, we were also making the decision on what to do with Oliver regarding schooling. He was way behind. His writing, at eleven, was like that of a **four-year-old** still, and despite us offering to buy a laptop for the school for him to use, they insisted that he had to write as that is what the curriculum stated. I said to the head teacher, **"Would you insist that a physically disabled child walk like all the others and deny them a wheelchair?"** They stuttered and couldn't answer. I was so angry. He was falling further and further behind at school and we were told that he needed to go to a special school. We really didn't want this and the whole stress of this along with work was really getting us down.

We started to visit some schools, both mainstream and specialist. The specialist schools were horrid. We had to lock the doors behind us to stop Oliver escaping. It was so upsetting; he just hated schools. The pupils there ranged from able and with learning and behavioural problems to being severely disabled mentally and, or physically. The schools were great, they did an amazing job, but we really didn't think this was right for Oliver. We knew he was underachieving due to the poor help he received at school.

We tried several mainstream schools, including the one that we had moved to the catchment area for. That school, our preferred choice, was a let down. We described Oliver and they said that there was no way they could take him and if they did he wouldn't have the right support. They were open as the new **SENCO (Special Educational Needs Co Ordinator)** had just started at the school and had noted that the **SEN** department wasn't up to the standard it should be due to poor investment. We tried the top school in the county, a prestigious school. **"No, I'm sorry, your child will just get bullied, we can't control that."** We tried another great school. They spoke just of statistics and grades and had no mention of **SEN**.

Then we found something different: a mainstream school, in an area we weren't keen on, but they spoke a lot about **SEN** and, even better, they didn't speak about the top pupils or the statistics. They spoke about ensuring that every child achieved their own specific and personal potential. We arranged a visit. We walked through the door and met the **SENCO**. This was different. She got Oliver immediately and engaged with him about dinosaurs. She gave him some fidget toys and paid attention to him. You could see that this woman got him, but it was immediate; she was so talented. Oliver left with some tools to help him too, including a wristband that was green on one side with a smiley face and said **'I'm OK'**. On the reverse side, it was red, with a sad face and said **'I'm not OK'**. Oliver wore it with pride.

The next day we picked Oliver up from school. The teacher called us over, **"Hi, we have taken this off Oliver today as it's school policy**

to not wear jewellery." I looked at her in disbelief. **"What do you mean jewellery? This is to help Oliver to communicate how he's feeling; another school gave it to him."** I was disgusted and angry. It boiled my blood. All those calls *Oliver did this, Oliver did that*, no support or anything, and a school had given him a tool to help him only for it to be taken off of him by a misinformed and uneducated teacher. The next day I was at the school demanding to see the headteacher. There was just a real lack of understanding. I could not get over the difference between this school and what I had experienced just a couple of days ago in another. Why was it so different? A little digging told me why: apparently, the average teacher studies for four years to qualify, of which half a day is dedicated to training on neurodiversity. That's half a day out of 460 days, a disgraceful **0.0342%** of their time.

When you then think about the number of neurodivergent children in a school, this is disgraceful. In fact, as I write this book, the **Department For Education** reports that **19.5%** of children are recipients of special educational needs in schools. No wonder we end up with so many children unemployed or moving into crime. Another statistic, from the **Criminal Justice Joint Inspection** report, estimated that **half of those entering prison** could be expected to have a **neurodivergent** condition. Dealing with all of this was so hard, but we carried on. I carried on with self help and reading to build me up stronger. I also carried on with the study and I carried on with trying to make a difference for others. It took my mind off the worry at home and gave me drive.

The Ability Network

Still struggling, with everything going on, I looked for help. I noted that in the business under the employee help section, there was nothing mentioned about **neurodiversity**. I spoke to a director about it, hiding the fact it was for me, under the guise that I was finding out about more help for my son. He explained that it was covered by mental health. I disagreed. I told them that mental health and neurodiversity are linked, but it doesn't always mean you had a mental health issue if you were neurodivergent, I had researched this thoroughly, they were wrong. I said, **"Are you automatically classed as depressed if you are Dyslexic?"** They agreed this was wrong and it started to become a mission for me to change the narrative in the business. I wanted to start to help people with what I was learning about. At this stage though, I just couldn't say out loud I was, in fact, **Autistic**—I hadn't had a diagnosis for one, but also, the stigma was huge.

Even with all of this going on, I carried on with my studies and in **January 2021** I finally passed my first professional exam, closely followed by another in the February, and another in the March. I was on fire.

In **May** of that year, a chance turned up to join the **Diversity and Inclusion Board** representing disability. I interviewed for it and got the role. The director interviewing me could see and hear the passion; it meant so much to me. It was a volunteer role alongside my day job, but it was a chance for me to make a difference for others. I started to build a team around me, talking about all kinds of disabilities and tried to encourage people to forget the *dis* and just think of the *ability*, let's **enable ability**. We created internal websites as sources of information that were not previously there and gave our disabled staff and customers a voice.

I was keen to get the business the status of a **Disability Confident** employer, a government-backed scheme, to show disabled talent that we were interested, and we got it. I had spoken to the CEO (Chief Executive Officer) and he approved. However, there was a blocker in HR that was adamant we were not going to be doing this. They insisted that they didn't want people with disabilities working certain areas of the business like distribution as they couldn't do the job. I wouldn't back down. I knew the CHRO (Chief HR Officer) was up for it. I knew the CEO was up for it, but I had to convince the **whole of the HR leadership team.** I went to work and created a document and I presented it to the HR Leadership. With a bit of debate and to the dismay of some, I got it through and we duly signed up. We changed the wording on our job adverts and we started to make the difference I wanted to see. I wanted to make the world of work a better place for my son and people like him. **This was personal!**

I worked relentlessly with a fantastic team. I was able to talk to the CEO and the whole executive board of the business and help them understand the benefits of the business in doing this. We held an event to launch our **'Ability'** network and as a part of this we held a round table discussion with myself and some other colleagues and also the then COO (Chief Operating Officer). This was about to be an amazing moment. The COO spoke openly for the first time ever in his career, about him being **Dyslexic**. This was a massive breakthrough; we were **normalising the conversation of neurodiversity** in the business.

We spoke about the power of **visualisation** and how the neurodivergent mind could visualise in great detail and that this was a strength. I used an example of how I built a **two-storey playhouse with a slide** in our garden. People loved it and asked me where I got the plans. I explained that there were none. I had visualised and calculated everything in my head, brought the materials and built it. I explained that in my mind's eye, almost hovering in front of me, I could visualise and build it all in my head. I could see everything split out like a computer-aided design (CAD) or the exploded view of an engine in a Haynes manual.

It was also during this conversation that I learnt from our COO that he used **colour overlays** on his computer screen. This enabled him to read better as the words seemed to be still on the screen. Without this, the letters would seem to move around and get jumbled, and he really struggled. This got me thinking, *how can I help others with this?* I got to work with the team. We enabled coloured note pads to be ordered and also got the IT department to allow every colleague to access a Google plugin that could allow anyone to change the colour of their computer screen or the text on it. I just loved helping others.

The Case Study Failure

I was now to sit the first of my **three-hour** case studies in order to become fully qualified. It would entail lots of work for the weeks prior to the exam, reading a **30-page document** on a fictional company, memorising facts about the company and the people that worked there, and learning about the industry the company was in. You would then need to answer three questions, all set as an email from a senior manager to you regarding something that had happened in the business. You would then have an agonising **six weeks** wait for the result. These were so different to the multiple-choice exams I had sat prior. I just found that the questions, in the form of emails, were so long and so detailed that by the time I had got to the end of the question, I had forgotten what the start of it was about. I just couldn't absorb it all and had to re-read and re-read the question, which then meant I ran out of time.

Added to this, I would read a question that would, for example, start along the lines of…**'J.Colgate Limited had recently…..'** and for some reason my mind would be visualising toothpaste. It's all I could think of. It was so apparent in my mind. I'd get it out of my mind, refocus, and go again, but I just struggled so much.

After an agonising **six-week** wait, I got my result. I had waited up until midnight for it. **It was a fail—a big fat FAIL.** I was gutted. I had worked so hard at it.

I asked a question on a CIMA Facebook Group about if anyone else had struggled with having to constantly re-read questions like I had and if anyone had got a diagnosis for any neurodivergent conditions that had allowed them more time to absorb the long questions. I wasn't expecting the attack I got from a fellow member. They laid into me, telling me that if I had **Autism**, it was a **ME** problem and that getting extra time amounted to nothing more than cheating and devaluing the exam. I was mortified, upset, and also felt a huge sense of injustice. I contacted **CIMA**, and they were amazing. I had an apology, the member was spoken to and educated on neurodiversity. That way they dealt with it was fantastic and CIMA has been so incredibly supportive ever since.

Chapter 17 - Stepping On Up

The Commercial Analyst

In **June 2021**, I was again asked to apply for another job as a **Commercial Finance Analyst**, supporting the commercial team by analysing sales, profit margin, and market share. I was to report to another manager as Sam was also to move to a different part of the business. This manager was also new to our business. I decided I had to take the opportunity—the more I learnt, the better.

Again, I just had to improve the processes I inherited. I could see waste and poor processes all through them. I worked tirelessly to change them and did. I calculated it had saved over **ten hours** per month of doing exactly what I could get a computer and spreadsheet to do for me. I also shared this with a new graduate, who had taken over the digital analyst part of my previous role as it was a further improvement of what I had done there. I completely rebuilt how we reported on market share, giving greater insight and speeding up the results for the board. I also rebuilt a broken process that looked at cost price inflation and sales price inflation, enabling us to grow our profit margin.

It wasn't all roses though, as I had once again come across a manager, not a leader. Before I go into this, I have no grudge and I don't blame them,we are all at different parts of our journey of self development. They micro-managed and constantly put me down to start with. Despite this, I was stronger than before, and I had some great techniques to help me cope. I was determined it wouldn't affect me this time; I was stronger and more resilient as I had pushed my personal development. There was also a huge pressure for me to drop my **D&I (Diversity and Inclusion)** work. It wasn't seen as important as the day job, but I just didn't get it—I had achieved loads, I could do both.

The D&I Fight and the Whack-a-Mole

I was so proud and committed to the D&I work though, and I always got my day job completed. I became a **go-to** person and had so many people reach out to me, all going through the same journey. I'd even had a branch manager, going through the same journey as myself. He was in a bad place and was in tears in his office. Just at the end of what he could cope with, I helped him, supported him, and pointed him in the right direction to help and support his family. I did have a lot of people reach out to me, so much so that in my own time I built a network group for parents of **neurodivergent** children, a place where they could speak openly, be understood, and support each other.

The **Ability Network** team and I worked so hard and really helped to change the narrative around disability. So much so, I was nominated for an award in the business at the annual conference and was shortlisted to the last three. The MD (Managing Director) asked me, during a live stream of the awards ceremony, how I had been nominated by someone from a small branch in the middle of nowhere in Wales. I stated that it was because I cared and I wanted to help as many people as I could and spread the message far and wide. The beautiful glass trophy sits above me on a shelf, a reminder of the hard work and resilience and pushing back despite opposition.

The issues at work continued despite me delivering over and above. I struggled, and the brain fog was getting worse. I continued to beat myself up and blame myself. Kerry had other views though. Kerry again repeated that she thought I may have been seen as a threat, as my manager was new to the business and I was achieving some great results in what I was doing. By this time I also had a huge network, not many people in the business hadn't heard of me. I couldn't believe this though I still didn't have the self confidence to ever consider that may be the case. With the brain fog coming down, I was starting to make the odd mistake—nothing huge, spelling mistakes etc., but all of it would be picked up in huge detail and I'd be told that I would never be an accountant if I didn't get this right and pay more attention to detail.

Everything was growing darker and darker. One day, I got the blame for something from my manager's manager, and I knew it wasn't me. I was so fed up with how I was treated that I spoke up. The reply I got wasn't what I expected. The then head of finance said, on a phone call, **"If you two don't stop this 'he said, she said' shit, you're both fucking sacked."** I felt sick. To me, this was the end; my dream was over. I also felt anger. I knew I could do this. I knew I was good at my job when people allowed me to be. It was just so damn unfair. The same senior leader had actually given me praise for my work just weeks before! I asked him for some support and some help. I said I needed some **neurodivergent** specific coaching. He said, **"Well, if we get you coaching, everyone will want it so, no, we can't do that, it will set a precedent."** I knew deep down this was wrong. I knew it was probably also illegal when it came to disability discrimination. I felt so much anger and frustration. Others weren't struggling like I was, so why should I miss out? I kept the anger and frustration within though. I knew it would affect my career if I didn't.

The Access to Work Breakthrough

I was starting to feel it all get on top of me so much so, on some days just putting my password in my laptop could be hard work. I failed a resit of my case study too. There were the issues with Oliver at school, and now we were also having problems with Joshua. I felt like I was constantly being battered at work. I honestly felt like a **whack-a-mole**, and I was still awaiting a diagnosis; it had now been a year. Life was getting me down, and it was getting dark. I tried to get as much help as I could. There just wasn't really much available. At this point, I still didn't believe that I had a disability. I still hate saying that now. I know that in the right environment, I thrive. I absolutely thrive. I am so motivated, but it's the actions of others and environments created for me that bring me down. I knew that, to some extent, this was my problem. I needed to learn to deal with it. I knew that if I pointed the finger at someone there were three pointing straight back at me. I had to do something, I just couldn't fail again, I had to work on myself.

In researching, I found a **government-backed** scheme called **Access To Work**. It would enable me to get some coaching and support and help me build resilience. There was no way the business would pay for this, I had to find my own way. I knew that if I wanted to grow and truly become an accountant, I was going to have to deal with situations and management like this. However, I also felt not worthy as I didn't see myself as having a disability, and I felt bad that I was using government funds to help my uselessness. However, I felt I had no choice.

It was a long, drawn-out process, but eventually I got funding, and I was put in touch with a business called **Genius Within**. I was to have a group coaching event for people that worked with me and for anyone in the wider teams to enable them to learn about neurodiversity, and I was to have a series of one-to-one coaching sessions.

The Elephant Revelation (The Gift)

The team event **online** happened first. It was so great that how my brain worked was being explained to people around me. In fact, a couple of people contacted me afterwards and realised it may be a reason for their struggles too. That was reassuring to know it wasn't just me, but also disturbing how many others I was starting to come across. Unfortunately, one of the main people I wanted, and needed to join, didn't join the call.

The most amazing part of this course, though, was when we were all asked to close our eyes and imagine an elephant. We did this for a few minutes, and then the host went around the room, one by one, asking everyone to describe their elephant. Some said it was just big and grey. Some described it in its surroundings. **I described it in rich detail: its wrinkles, eyelashes, etc. I could see it vividly in HD, right there in my mind's eye.** Another person was embarrassed that they couldn't actually visualise anything at all, that they knew an elephant was big and grey, but they couldn't actually create a picture of it in their mind. **This amazed me. In fact, it was such a revelation I actually felt a bit of emotion over it.** *Is this why people had asked me to create those dashboards? Is this why I thought people were lazy and just putting on me?* It wasn't the case at all, although in some cases it may have been. But it made me understand, truly understand, that our brains are all uniquely different. None of us have the same set of skills, and some of the skills **neurodivergent** people have are exceptional. **These are skills you cannot learn; these are skills that you are born with—a gift.** Yes, we have so many struggles if we are in the wrong environment, but get this right and we can do amazing things.

It wasn't long after this that the relationship with my manager was about to change. We had a scoring matrix that was used in the business to help with self development. My manager was trying. However, the comments, in my opinion, just didn't align with me. It mentioned nothing of the achievements I had. It was predominantly negative. I couldn't settle that evening, so I sent an email to her explaining my frustration and with examples of everything I had achieved. I agreed I still had lots I needed to develop on, but my scoring was that of a junior, the lowest you could get in some areas. I felt so much injustice. The next day we met in the office. I could see she was not happy, not at all. We went into a meeting room, and she lost it with me: **"You've stressed me out! I couldn't sleep last night because of you."** I decided to speak up. I told her how I felt for the first time. I let it all out. I thought, *I can't take it anymore*. I didn't care if I was to get sacked, so be it, but I just can't keep this inside anymore. I hated conflict. It made my stomach churn. It made me feel physically sick.

After that day, things started to change. My manager began to support me more, became more understanding, and by the time I was to leave this role, we got on fine. In fact, we are still in contact now. I don't hold a grudge and I know that when you point a finger, there are three pointing back at you, and I do take some blame. I should have had the courage to speak up sooner. I also now think more about what the manager is going through—they could well be having stuff go on in their lives too—but when you are in a dark place and you are made to feel such injustice, that can be hard. My manager became so supportive, and the relationship started to build. My brain fog disappeared and my work got back to standard. My manager also coached me with my case study and taught me techniques. They had actually been an exam marker for CIMA before.

The Conference and Finding My Tribe

I was so keen to make a difference around Neurodiversity that I started to volunteer for a charity called Neurodiversity In Business. I helped a little with accounts, but then also helped them to organise their first ever conference. It was to be at the Excel Centre in London, and I wanted to represent the business I worked for and was so proud of. With what had been happening though, I didn't want to ask for time off or expenses for the day of the conference, so I took annual leave and paid for my own travel.

The day was amazing. I had never spent a day with people that actually got me like this before. It was like I had known these people for years. **It was like I had finally found people that spoke my language—just such an unreal feeling**. I know what it was: **we were all neurodivergent**. In a world of **iPhones and Androids**—systems that talk a different language—we were all **Androids**. We truly got each other; it was so life-affirming. Apart from Kerry, there were only two other people that I had this connection with: **Paul and Bunter**. Paul was **neurodivergent**; he was **Dyslexic**. And Bunter—the clown, the joker, the one full of energy and life and mischief—well, he was diagnosed with **ADHD** later in life. It's no coincidence. We got on because we were all wired differently. I have gone on to find this so often, there are so many people out there that I just get a feeling are neurodivergent, I seem to just hit it off with them and then discover they have a diagnosis. In fact, 9 times out of 10, when networking, if I go up to someone who is standing alone looking awkward and get talking to them, I find out they have a diagnosis. On the other hand, there are many that I really struggle with that have no diagnosis, but more to the point, no self awareness.

There was one thing I did struggle with though, and it was on this day I would find out why and find some solutions to help. When I was in a busy place, I always struggled to hear; I would have to **lip-read** people. This actually helped with eye contact too: I would look at people's mouths, but they would assume I was looking at them toward their eyes, I hope. It seemed that in places like this, all the noise **blended into one**, and I struggled to pick out a single voice. This was another **Autistic trait**, and in the goody bags were a sample set of **Flare earplugs**. They were a small silicone cone that you pop, unnoticed, in your ear, and it helped somewhat with **zoning in** on a conversation—not perfect, but they certainly **helped** a little.

The Final Miracle

Life was about to take another turn, as it often did for us. Kerry was pregnant again, a total shock as we had used no contraception for over **eight years** since Joshua was born, as Kerry and I wanted a girl. It just wasn't happening though due to her condition. I was elated, but shocked. I was now 44. I felt I was too old to be a dad again. When the time came for the scan where we could find out the sex, we walked in, hand in hand, so apprehensive as to what we might hear. We were happy we were having another baby. All we wanted was for them to be healthy, but deep down we desperately wanted a girl. When the sonographer asked if we wanted to know the sex, we agreed. We gripped each other's hand tighter in sheer anticipation...**"It's a girl."** We were over the moon, so happy. There were tears of joy. This was such amazing news.

We decided we wanted to surprise the boys, and we wanted them to be the first to know, so we went and **bought** a huge pink party popper full of pink confetti. After school that day, we were so excited, and we gathered them together in the hallway. **"OK boys, we are going to find out if mummy has a boy or a girl in her belly! Are you excited?"**

"Yes, yes," they said, jumping up and down. Together we excitedly pulled the string, and pink confetti went everywhere. We jumped with joy, except the boys didn't. They went off in a huff saying, **"We don't want a girl."** What a let down! We laugh about it now, but we found that hard.

Chapter 18 - The Genius Within

Oliver Finds His Environment

September 2021: Oliver was starting at secondary school. It didn't go well for the first few months. We had to take him to reception, often kicking and screaming, and they would lock the door behind him. They would then take him to a quiet area called **'The Base'**. This was in a lower level of the school and out of the way; it was a haven and a safe space for **SEN** students. He had some struggles, he had some bullying, but the school worked as a team with us and were brilliant. It was so different from the experience at junior school; they actually got it and they actually cared. Eventually Oliver didn't need to be restrained. He wanted to go to school; he began to enjoy it. The difference? **The environment created for him and the understanding.**

It did take some while for the school to get the funding for him, though. The local authority had lost his paperwork and we had to submit it all over again! The school was amazing, though, and gave him what he needed anyway while they waited.

The Spiky Profile

It was now time to start my coaching. I had booked a meeting room at work and planned to meet the coach in reception, a lady we will call Claire. I nervously met her at reception and took her to the meeting room. I was really apprehensive. Claire was amazing; she got it. This was the first time I had spoken to someone that had really got it; they totally understood me. We went to work over the course of the following weeks and months, and it was Claire that really helped me truly understand that I was just **different and not broken**.

We started with a test, a bit like the **Insights** test that was computer based and just asked a number of questions—no right or wrong answer, just go with how you felt. It rated me extremely high at problem solving, visual and practical skills, organisation, written word, numerical skills, and dexterity. Communication and memory and concentration I was at about 50%. However, it was no surprise that interpersonal skills and managing my state scored zero. **Embarrassing, but true—I just struggled despite all the work I had done on self development.**

I had good grounding as I already knew a fair bit about **neurodiversity**. I had also found, through lockdown, that a quieter environment helped me to focus and I didn't have the social awkwardness to deal with. Claire asked me if I had heard of the **spiky profile**. It was something that was totally new to me. There was a visual representation of it and Claire described it to me. It showed all of the different skills along one axis and then the scores for an individual were plotted along the graph. In the example, you could see that a **neurotypical** person would normally score an average, and that **neurodivergent** people mostly scored really high on some areas and really low on others, just like the results from my test and thus creating a spiky line along the graph.

We then started to run through my strengths, my big wins. There were many, but I was ashamed to talk about them. Talking about them last time just got me hit down with the comment, **"Well if you read that you would think you were the saint of [company name redacted]"**. I also didn't want to come across as someone with an ego; that really concerned me, it always had. We then discussed my weaknesses. To me, there were many; they far outweighed any strengths. These were my main focus. I just wanted to be better. I just wanted people to like me. We spoke about many things and even went back to the past, where many of the problems started. I was constantly told I was useless at school and by my parents. I had always struggled to make friends. I just wanted so desperately to be liked and to feel like I fit in. I mentioned that I felt lonely; even in a room full of people I could feel so damn lonely. I had covered this in the book called **The Courage To Be Disliked** before but it had just not sunk in as it should have. These thoughts that are drummed into you as a child are hugely damaging and it takes an immense amount of work to improve your self worth.

We worked on so many strategies to help me and I worked so hard at it. I didn't want to be a pain. I just wanted to be understood, to be able to do my best work, and to be recognised and treated with respect.

Some of these techniques and lessons were so life changing, but I just thought, ***why wasn't I taught this at school?*** Instead of learning how my brain worked, I learnt how to shade with a pencil, what the date of the **Battle Of Hastings** was, how to measure the discharge rates or flow of a river, the works of **Shakespeare**, and a really twisted view of the history of Britain. **No one, not one teacher, taught me how my brain works**, how to find my strengths, how to find strategies to help with my weaknesses, how to build relationships, how to deal with finances, how to communicate effectively, or how to learn well and get the best out of myself. No, we were battered with information we might not ever use again and made to feel useless. This brought up lots of emotions. I felt rage and injustice at how I'd been brought up; how my parents, the education system and health service had let me down.

The Chimp Paradox

I also learned that I was my worst enemy as I wanted nothing more than perfection from myself. If I ever gave anything other than 100%, I would beat myself up. I hated myself if I got bad feedback or I did something wrong. It would have a profound physical effect on me. I learnt that this was called **RSD (Rejection Sensitivity Dysphoria)**. It is a known trait of those with **ADHD**. An example of this would be a manager asking me if they could see me later for five minutes. For the rest of the day I would be so anxious that I had done something wrong that I would feel physically sick. I would also learn that by this time, many diagnosis of Autism or ADHD were dual and covered them both, with many people calling it **AuDHD**

This is when a life changing book was mentioned: ***The Chimp Paradox*** by Steve Peters. The Chimp Paradox presents a simple model for understanding the mind, dividing it into three main parts: the **Chimp** (the emotional, impulsive, and irrational part of your brain), the **Human** (the logical, rational thinking part of your brain), and the **Automatic Brain** (the memory bank for beliefs and habits and experiences). The "paradox" is that your inner Chimp can be both your best friend and your worst enemy, often hijacking your thoughts and actions. The book teaches you to recognise when your Chimp is in charge, learn to soothe and manage its emotional outbursts, and empower your rational Human side to make better decisions. This book was the base of the mental training for the **2012 Olympic cycling team** including **Chris Hoy, Bradley Wiggins, and Victoria Pendleton** and enabled them to keep the emotion at bay and concentrate all of their energy on the task in hand. It worked. The team won eight gold medals out of a possible ten and went down as one of the best Olympic cycling teams in the world. They put much of this down to the knowledge gained from the Chimp Paradox.

This is where I really learnt about the environments I had put myself in or found myself in throughout the years. Because of being, at this time, potentially **Autistic**, my Chimp was rattling his cage and making himself known through emotional turmoil. I needed to learn to calm my Chimp. In the case of a manager asking me to attend a meeting later with no notice of what it was about, I could set things in place to stop this, just by having the confidence to ask my manager to always talk to me straight away and not leave me hanging. That would be a reasonable adjustment.

It was clear to me that I had years and years of bad experience built up in the education system and by the narrative of those around me that had compounded negative thoughts in my head. Every time my Chimp got rattled, my Automatic Brain would use a past experience to work out what was going on. What I needed to do was bring in rational thinking. Was there evidence of what I was thinking? Was it true, or was it just a combination of my Chimp and my Automatic Brain? It wasn't easy; it took a lot of practice and I still visit it all of the time.

I have to say, this book changed my life! Now, when I have an emotional impact, such as an email that really winds me up, I have to work to take the emotion out of it. If I need to, I walk away and do something else to distract my Chimp. When I'm calm, I can then use my rational Human brain to absorb it properly and come up with a response with less emotion. Okay, I didn't always get it right. Sometimes you have to write the email and walk away and not send it at all until days later. I have come to the conclusion that none of us can be perfect. Perfection does not exist. All we can do is to do our best and learn from our mistakes.

Learning about what rattled my Chimp's cage was interesting too. There was lack of sleep and tiredness; if I was tired it became irritated. I learnt, though, that tiredness for an **Autistic** person might not equal lack of sleep. Our minds do not switch off. We have a powerful inner monologue. We constantly think about what might happen. We prepare conversations in our heads over and over again. We then beat ourselves up because we hadn't ended up saying what we had practised because we couldn't get it out. We visualise constantly, planning our every move to perfection, then analyse our failures over and over and over again. This is draining. Being **Autistic** is hard work, but hard work that no one sees.

Claire helped me enormously over those sessions and we still keep in touch, but not on a professional basis. **Thank you!**

It shouldn't be that we end up in a crisis and then a business pays thousands for a course. We should be taught this in schools to prepare us for life. It would help everyone, not just those who are **Autistic** or **neurodivergent**. I truly believe every manager should be taught this too. Far too many businesses promote people that are good at their jobs into management roles, but there is no qualification to start managing people. It takes four years to qualify as a teacher or an accountant. There is no official training to manage people, and getting it wrong can not only impact the profit of a business, it can also ruin lives.

The Final Exams

After two failed attempts at the exam and armed with some newfound tools for success, it was now time to take another resit of this dreaded three-hour case study. I prepared so hard. The pressure was off at work now my manager and I were working better together and I had these strategies in place. I used the techniques my manager had taught me along with keeping control of my Chimp. I was to find the actual question part first—what was the ask—then I was to pull out the facts given to me. I would then recall the facts I had learnt in the pre-reading and apply my understanding of the subject to write the answer. These were expected to be long, detailed answers, but without going into technicalities of accounting. You were to treat them more like a task at work.

I used the techniques. It was still hard, but it wasn't meant to be easy. I waited patiently for another **six weeks** for the result. The night had come and I waited up for the result. I waited and waited, so anxious just hoping and praying I would pass this time. If not, I really felt like I was going to give up. I even thought about going back and driving a truck. I fell asleep, my phone in my hand. Around one o'clock I woke up and realised it was time. My heart was racing. I felt sick with anxiety and clicked the link…**PASS!** Yes, I had finally passed and was on to the next level, the Management level. My designatory letters changed from **CIMA Cert BA** to **CIMA Dip. MA**. I now had just eight exams to go to become a fully qualified chartered accountant.

Maia's Arrival

In **April 2022**, our miracle daughter was born. We named her **Maia**, the goddess of spring. It was on the way to a hospital check up, not long before she was born, that we saw the beautiful spring blossoms on a row of cherry blossom trees along the roadside and this prompted that beautiful name. She was and is amazing, so small. We had forgotten just how small a newborn was—our perfect little daughter.

Oliver was doing amazingly at school too. In his first year, he had caught back up with his grades. He had won a distinction in an **Oxford University BEBRAS** challenge and won the Principal's award for his outstanding attendance and behaviour. He even became a buddy for other **SEN** students joining the school. He was like a different boy, all because they understood him and created an environment where he could thrive. We were so pleased with him, as was the school.

It wasn't all great though. We often thought we had done something massively wrong in a previous life, and life constantly threw us lemons. We had no support from family. In fact, we had become the **black sheep**, the ones with a big house and problem children. Ever since we had moved into a larger house in a nice part of town, we started to see less of people, and we could see we were treated differently. We were on a journey though. We had left anyone negative behind. We didn't need them in our lives. We had each other, and that's all we needed, but, god, life was tough.

The School Conflict

There was a new head teacher at the primary school, and things were changing. Joshua wasn't coping at all. She was not someone who believed in **neurodiversity**. In her opinion, kids should sit still and be quiet and learn. Well, they should, but if they are not, you need to understand why and help them deal with it. We'll come to that later.

One Friday, Oliver had gone with Kerry to collect Joshua from school. He had a great relationship with one of the teachers and they talked about **Pokemon**. He was the only teacher at that school he had ever liked, a bit like my Mrs. Cooper. Every Friday without fail they would talk about **Pokemon** while we waited for Joshua. The new head teacher decided that every Friday she would take a loudspeaker and play music on full volume in the playground at the end of the day. It really was loud—you could hear it down the street as you approached. Oliver approached the headteacher and asked if she could turn it down. It was hurting his ears and too loud. She told him not to be so rude and he didn't go to that school so go away. Kerry was furious. **"My son is Autistic, he kindly asked you to turn it down as it was physically hurting his ears,"** she replied.

"Well, he needs to learn to cope. I enjoy the music. The kids enjoy the music and I won't be turning it down," she replied. He wasn't the only one though. It seems a few people struggled, and the local residents complained to the council. Within a few weeks it was gone! With an attitude like that, it was no wonder Joshua was struggling.

We worked so hard to try and work with the school. They were terrible. The issues just didn't stop and visits to the school were endless. I tried to bring some of the tools I used in business into the conversation. For example, I said that if Joshua or another child does something wrong that they just deal with the action they had seen. However, that was just a **'sticking plaster'** solution as this wasn't always the cause. In business we use the **5 Whys method** to find the root cause. This says that if you keep asking *why*, on average, within five times you will find the root cause.

I'll give you an example. A child is calling out, interrupting and tapping their pencil on the desk. Most schools and teachers would call the child out in front of the class. This would incite embarrassment. The child would do it again, and then the teacher would discipline the child, often by sending them to reset, in a quiet room or making them stay behind for detention. How about this? We ask why the child is doing that, stay with me. It turns out they have been tasked with reading a challenging textbook chapter. The child in question has finished early and is bored. ***Why are they bored?*** They found it way too easy and not engaging and once finished there was no other task. They struggled to sit still with such an active mind. ***Why was there no other task?*** The teacher had planned a lesson for the class as a whole and expected them to finish all at the same time. ***Why?*** The teacher hadn't realised that this child was exceptionally gifted and had trouble sitting still. It was impossible for them. They were diagnosed with **ADHD**. ***Why hadn't the teacher realised this?*** The teacher had no training on **neurodivergent** conditions and followed a rule that every child should learn in the same way. So by not getting to the root cause, we had disciplined a gifted child and ridiculed them in front of the class, making them even less engaged in their lessons. Had the **'5 Whys'** been employed, OK, only 4 in this case, the child could have been given a task as a back up task for every time they had completed their work before anyone else, or been moved into a higher class. Instead of the teacher realising their gift, they were seen as a problem.

This is how we end up with so many children out of work or moving into the criminal justice system. We are disciplining that child because they are gifted but can't sit still. Remember the story of **Gillian Lynne**, the little girl that couldn't sit still in class, was seen as naughty and taken to the doctor. The doctor asked the *whys*, got to the root cause and helped her Mum realise she needed a different learning environment. She succeeded and became a millionaire. That isn't just luck or chance; that's the power of creating the right environment. I had begun to learn through my lived experience and through my continued learning that the environment was everything. Think about this: you plant a rose in a desert and it wilts and dies. You plant it in a cottage garden and give it nutrients, and it thrives. The thing is, though, we are not all roses and if we were, life would be boring. We learnt from the talk I mentioned about visualising an elephant that we are all entirely different. Yet we sit 30 children in a classroom and expect them to learn the same way and think and behave the same way. We are trying to hammer **square pegs into round holes**, and, through my experience in how I have struggled, you can clearly see that is damaging.

The Final Leap

Back at work and study and things were going well. The manager I didn't get on with even recommended me for an exciting new role helping to embed a brand new finance system for the whole business. Again, I got the job. I had a lot of experience in the data of the business; it was a perfect fit. I was now the conduit between the operators of the business and a large team of engineers in India and was tasked with creating all of the new reporting for the business, from branch level reports, right up to CEO level. It was great. I took the whole workstream from sorting and cleansing data, writing the requirements, running workshops to ascertain the exact requirements from varying departments in the business, providing a feedback loop to the Indian team through to starting to deliver the reports.

I was continuing my studies too. I passed the first exam with no problem, but then hit another wall. The questions were longer and more detailed. I could answer them, but it just took me so long to absorb them, just re-reading and re-reading. I often questioned if I should give it up, but I had got this far, I wasn't quitting. I approached CIMA to see if I could get an allowance of extra time or a separate room. I'd previously had an argument go on in the background during one exam; it was so hard to concentrate. I was told that there was no chance of this as I didn't have a diagnosis. I felt injustice as I knew I could pass these exams; I just needed a little extra time to absorb the questions, and the right environment, that was all. I was now over three years into awaiting a diagnosis. I had started the process and had spent hours talking through the issues. I was so close. Another few exams failed later and I was about to give up. It just felt impossible.

Chapter 19 - The Diagnosis

The Verdict

Finally, a few months later, Kerry and my Dad had now been interviewed by the **NHS Adult ADHD, Autism and Tourette's Team** about my history, what I was like as a person, and what I was like as a child. I received a letter to say they had an outcome, and I would have a call at 9am on **March 9th, 2023**. I felt huge anxiety. ***Was I, wasn't I? Was there a reason for the way I was, or was I just broken? Am I a fraud?*** It was all going through my head—a whole **rollercoaster** of emotions.

The day came. The practitioner called. She spoke through her findings and told me that she had no uncertainty about her decision. She said, **"It is therefore my clinical opinion that you have a diagnosis of an Autism Spectrum Disorder, present since childhood."**

I couldn't hold back the tears. It was like a tonne weight had just been lifted off my shoulders. I literally felt lighter at that moment. It was immense. The world suddenly made sense. I wasn't broken. **"I AM NOT FUCKING BROKEN! I AM NOT FUCKING BROKEN!"** I cried out to myself after the call, the tears just rolling. Despite me going from being adamant I was autistic and then adamant I wasn't, then I was again, I finally had clarity, undeniable proof. I wasn't stupid. I wasn't an idiot. I didn't just go to the wrong school, I didn't just eat the wrong diet, I wasn't anything less than anyone else. I was me. My brain was just wired differently.

Everything suddenly made sense, but yet, my emotions were a ball of confusion. I struggled. I had anger that school and my parents didn't realise over all of these years. I had anger that I didn't realise over all of these years of suffering. I still had doubts that I wasn't autistic as on so many days, in fact the majority, I was fine. It was just the environments that people created for me or that I put myself in that I just couldn't handle. I was a rose that needed to **find my cottage garden** and **not try to survive in a desert.**

The Ticking Clock

I wrote to **CIMA** about my diagnosis. It took forever to get a response, but they gave me **25% extra reading time** and a **quiet individual room**. I hurriedly went to book my next exam, but I couldn't. Because I had permission for my own quiet room. I had to book it on the phone. It was a drawn out process, it was another hoop to jump through, but I did it.

I turned up for the exam. I had worked so hard. This was it. I was given a chance; I had to pass. I had some foam ear plugs given to me. We went through the usual ID checks and pre-exam procedures, and I was shown the room. I headed over, a tiny little room, a chair and a desk, nicely painted, it was perfect. Apart from **the most huge and loud ticking clock, right above my head!** I tried to get it out of my head as I worked, but it seemed so loud ringing in my ears: ***tick, tick, tick, tick***. It was driving me crazy. I had been given a room that was quiet so that I wasn't distracted, but they had given me an environment that was even more distracting just through lack of knowledge. I tried and I tried, I had the ear plugs in, I put on the supplied headphones, nothing. It was so damn **LOUD**, echoing around my brain. I just could not absorb the questions. The ticking was just so loud in my head. The **vice-like pressure** building up in my temples. *I can't do this,* I thought, *I just can't do this*. I felt so much injustice. I had found a way that would help me, and it was like there was absolutely no care or understanding. Why would they put me in a room so I could have quiet and concentrate but with a loud repetitive sound. I was angered.

I stood up and walked out to the invigilator. **"I can't do this,"** I said, **"I think I'll just have to give up."**

"Wait, what's the problem?" The invigilator could see I was totally stressed out. **"You have given me a quiet room but with the loudest ticking clock right above my head, I just can't concentrate, I just can't do this."** The team was great. They calmed me down, removed the clock, and I decided to carry on. The time had not stopped though; the exam was still running, and I had lost a chunk of time. I took a while to refocus and used my breathing technique, blowing out the frustration, the anger, the noise echoing around my head, that thick black smoke, and I took a deep breath in, a breath of confidence, a breath of light and goodness and I went to work.

I worked so hard in that exam, but I just didn't feel I had done enough. I had extra time, but a majority of that was used up with the clock fiasco. I came out exhausted and deflated, I had given it everything, I couldn't afford to fail this time, it was stretching us financially paying for resits. After the usual checks, the lady handed me the piece of paper: **PASS**. I was over the moon and so relieved yet still felt so much injustice and lack of care, it was like no one listened and boxes were just ticked for the sake of doing so. However, another one in the bag! There were now just two more to go to finish this level.

Over the coming months, I passed the next multiple choice exam and the case study for that level. I now had an **Advanced Diploma in Management Accounting, CIMA Adv. Dip. MA.**

The Next Pivot

The new role was going okay. My secondment was coming to an end though, and I was speaking to my mentor about next steps. I told him my desire. He told me no one would pay me that. I had a conversation with an internal recruiter and they said something similar. He said, **"You have been here so long that the only way to get more money would be to leave and come back."** I was gobsmacked. That didn't make financial sense for the business: they would have to advertise, interview and train someone else and it would take years to build the business knowledge and connections I had. I found it so frustrating. Why would a business not invest in knowledge and experience and pay me what I could get elsewhere and what my fellow colleagues were getting? I felt injustice. I had been in the business for over eight years. I had worked from the shopfloor stacking shelves to now working at the head office, part of a team installing a new finance system. I had knowledge and experience in supply chain, distribution, and branches, and was almost fully qualified as an accountant. I still felt like an imposter though; I still didn't feel good enough.

I also saw that the business was changing and not for the better. They had changed their external image and advertising. To me, it just didn't work, and I could see that the market share was falling. To me they weren't talking to the right people in the external media. It was all about politics and policy and pictures outside of **Number 10**, all aimed at the big corporate house builders that bought in bulk but at a low price. Meanwhile, competitors were still appealing to the generalist builder, the people that had to work to pay their mortgage and couldn't just mothball a large site like the major house builders. They also paid higher prices leading to greater profits; it's how all businesses work. Added to this there were still issues with product data, particularly units of measure, and I had reported several times that it needed to be fixed before we went to the new system. I said that putting the old data and old units of measure in a new system was like buying a new fishtank and then pouring the old dirty water in it. All you get is the same data, but in an expensive system. In my mind, we had to fully cleanse and sort the base data before we moved on.

One day we had a presentation for **International Women's Day**. The Director in charge of the project presented her own journey and drew a graph of a man's career journey versus a woman's. The man's career journey had a constant upward trajectory; it was plain sailing, but women struggled. I agreed. I have always been a massive advocate of women in business and always will be, and women have been my best managers by far. However, I felt that I wasn't represented. Yes, it was International Women's Day and it certainly wasn't about me, but this was someone telling me, in my head, that I had it easy. **I'd had it far from easy.** We spoke afterwards and she agreed. She probably shouldn't have stereotyped, and we spoke in more detail about her career and her **imposter syndrome** she had mentioned. I was keen to learn more about how she had achieved what she had and she invited me to put an hour in her diary for a catch up. I asked her in our meeting, **"What got you through thinking you weren't good enough?"** She said that an ex-manager had told her, **"Don't go for jobs you know you can do easily. Stretch yourself. You may make some errors, but you will grow, you will learn, and then do it again. Keep on pushing and doing what you once thought you couldn't."** I got this as I knew that by talking publicly more and more and presenting at a top level more and more it was getting easier. The same with my running too: the more I pushed, the further I could go. But to apply for a job that I didn't think, in my mind, I was confident to do just didn't seem right.

I took this away and thought deeply about it. I was stuck here on much lower pay than my fellow colleagues. I was doing a good job, in fact, looking back, I was doing a great job, but I was told I wouldn't ever get paid what I was worth if I stayed. This hurt. I loved this business, I never really wanted to leave and would still go back now. I needed more though. I needed to pay off my debts I had incurred on this journey and I needed to give my family more as I had been working so hard and they weren't seeing the benefits. I started to look for another job. I had several interviews, but wasn't successful. I was open about my Autistic diagnosis in all applications. I wanted people to know the real me so I could work in an environment where I would work best. I applied for jobs with businesses that were part of the **Disability Confident Scheme.** My experience of that was that they had just done it as a tick box exercise, they could in no way create the right environment. One of them, a household name, even told me I didn't get the job as I didn't have enough Excel experience. I had bags of it! I used to teach others. Besides, they didn't even ask me about Excel in the interview. Then, suddenly, a job advert came along for an American-owned business. It was a small business, privately owned, but had an office about an hour away and a factory up in the north of England. I interviewed for the role of **Management Accountant**. I was open about my diagnosis and that I was pushing to the next level. There would be tasks I would be new at. I wanted to push, but also be fully open and transparent. To my surprise, I got the job, and the salary was nearly double what I was currently on. My mentor was wrong!

I handed my notice in, and the next day I went to the office. I saw the director that had given me the advice. **"You dickhead,"** she said laughing, **"why are you leaving us? Please don't leave us."**

"I'm sorry," I said, **"I took your advice. I want to push to the next level and I want a proper salary."**

"Hey, I don't blame you," she said, **"you will be amazing, we will all really miss you."**

The Toxic Workplace

In **August 2023** I left. I was really gutted. I absolutely loved this company, but I was frustrated that no one could see the issues I could and that I was earning less than everyone else. I still miss this business dearly. I wouldn't be where I am today without the development I got there and I am so thankful for it. Yes, there were some dark times, but I always felt supported apart from a few individuals, and I had gone from stacking dusty shelves to where I was now. It was a huge part of me.

I was to work in the office three days a week in my new role, Tuesday, Wednesday, and Thursday, with Monday and Fridays at home. I was told that I'd be fully supported and that the tasks I wasn't used to would be shown to me and I would soon pick it up. The first day was a Monday, but I was to go into the office. It was just the manager and myself in the whole office, a very strange atmosphere, but I did like the quiet. We spent the day trying to get me on to the IT systems, but it was like wading through mud, and I left the first day having done nothing.

The next day, I went in and met the team and finally got logged on. As I started to get to know the people, I started to feel uneasy. The way the manager spoke to the women there was terrible. **"You women, you are all the same, shut up and do some work, stop gabbling."** It was supposedly banter; it was daily. When he wasn't around, the women would go on about him, it was constant backstabbing. All I wanted to do was get on with my work. There was a lot of it too. I tried to just knuckle down and switch off to it. I was given the balance sheets to reconcile; they hadn't been done in over six months. They were a mess! The manager disappeared up North. I mentioned that he said he would show me the ropes. **"No, I am not good at teaching. I thought you'd be better off jumping in at the deep end."** I panicked. I couldn't just leave these documents in a mess. Everything was totally wrong, nothing aligned. It was just a big muddle. Not only that, I had also been given France, Italy, and Germany to look after and I had never dealt with foreign currency apart from in my studies. I hated getting things wrong and I liked things right and in order. I worked relentlessly over the coming months to try and bring it around. I completely rebuilt all of the processes, rebuilt all of the balance sheets with fresh data, put in checks and controls, and sorted out the tangle, which I found went back over four years! I also found out they had been through a string of Management Accountants. So I wasn't surprised by the mess.

The office was toxic and moody. Hardly anyone spoke all day. They would just sit there with long faces, typing away. No one took a lunch break. I tried to get them to come on a lunch walk; no one was interested, all tied to their desks. The quietness I liked, though, and it allowed me to **hyperfocus** on the tasks. When there was conversation, though, it was just gossip and vileness. I sat there one day with the woman opposite saying she would never let her daughter date a black person, and using a hugely offensive word. I spoke up about it, I was disgusted. I have many Black and Asian friends. There was no way I was listening to that and keeping quiet.

One day I got called into the office by the manager. **"What the fuck have you done Gavin?"**

"I don't know, what do you mean?"

"There is a post you put on LinkedIn. You have mentioned how working at home is good for people and that neurodivergent people work better from home. The CEO has gone mad as he wants everyone to go back to the office full time. You better take it down; you have a target on your back now." He told me I had to read the company policy on social media and that my LinkedIn account was only for work use. I was to stop posting anything other than sales related content for the business. By this time, I had almost **3,000 followers** on **LinkedIn** and was becoming a thought leader in the area of **neurodiversity in business**. I was fuming, angry inside, but didn't want to lose my job. I read the company policy. He was right. An **eight-page** document stating that social media, even if it is a personal account, must only be used for purposes of benefit to the business.

I was really not feeling this place, and I knew, if I stayed in an environment like this, I would go down hill, fast. I was a rose in a desert. I set about finding something else.

Chapter 20 - The Final Destination, or is it?

The Dream Job

During a scan of **LinkedIn**, I saw that **Jennifer** was now working for one of the world's leading motoring manufacturers—one I really admired. In fact, I had models of their cars I lined up as a child, and my Dad was an absolute fanatic about one of their cars from the 1960s; it was and had always been his dream car. I popped Jennifer a note. Jennifer replied, **"Hi Gav, it's so great to hear from you. I think you would be a really good fit for this role. If you would like me to, I would be happy to put a recommendation in for you."** I jumped at the chance, even if it was well over an hour's drive to the office, as it was a hybrid role of an average of two days in the office.

A week or so later, I got invited to one of their prestigious sites. I was in my element, with my history in the motor trade and my absolute love of cars. I was so excited about this. The time came, and I popped on my suit and drove over an hour and a half to the site where I was to be interviewed. There were three people there, all taking notes, and with a stream of questions. Again, I was fully open about my diagnosis. I was asked loads of technical questions around budgeting, forecasting, and cashflow. I answered them all with little hesitation—this was my passion. I still thought that I wouldn't have a chance though. I still had some doubts, that damn **imposter syndrome**, and all the way home after the interview, it went around and around in my head: ***Was I enough? Did they like me?*** For a couple of weeks, radio silence. I knew it was too good to be true. **This is a global giant, one of the UK's largest businesses; they would never want me, an ex-dustman that left school with no qualifications.**

I got a call. **"Hi, Gavin, it's the recruitment team here from [name redacted]. I have some news for you about your application."** I felt sick with dread. They were about to say thank you but no thank you. **"I'm pleased to say, the interviewers were impressed with you at the interview and they would like to offer you the role."** I couldn't believe it. Wow, little old me, working for this absolute giant. I tried to hold back my excitement the best I could. **"We will send you a proposal via email. If you could read it and confirm you are happy, we can then progress you through to the onboarding stage."** I was so happy about this; Kerry and I jumped for joy. My Dad was in disbelief. This was epic. It was later that I discovered that there were 45 candidates for the role. It made me proud that with my background, I had achieved this.

I was about to drive to work on my first day there. I was absolutely filled with pride as I got into my car. I had never felt so good. On the way, I thought about all those people along the way that put me down and didn't believe in me. I felt like a winner. I felt on top of the world. I had a huge smile on my face all the way there, despite also being nervous. I met my new manager at the security office at the visitors entrance. The place was out of this world; the site was huge. We headed to the main building and reception and went through the revolving doors. It opened up into a huge atrium of glass. The place was vast; it was like an airport or a shopping hall. I looked across to my right and there was the exact car my dad had always dreamed of, sat there on display. Everywhere we looked there were exhibits; it was like a motor museum. The hairs stood up on my neck and I held my head up with pride! At last, I felt I had made it. **I was an Accountant. I wasn't useless. I wasn't a failure. I was me, and I was proud to be me!**

I would end up stepping up in the original role after less than a year, and at the time of writing this book, I am a **Finance Business Partner** looking after 12 Directors of the business covering prototype engineering, strategy, and launch with a budget of **£50m** and over 800 colleagues. I have also had the privilege of driving their cars. I was in my element doing that.

The Graduation

During my time here, I also passed my final exams and I am now officially a Chartered Global Management Accountant and I proudly have a plaque on my office wall, right in front of me, so that in times of self doubt, I can remind myself of my achievements. I am Gavin Simpson ACMA CGMA and I am worthy of it. I would eventually take

Kerry and my Dad to a new members' ceremony in London where I was presented with a scroll for my qualification in a graduation style ceremony. We had some great photos of me with my Dad and with Kerry and also receiving my scroll. I cherish these. I didn't go to university, I didn't have that picture on the wall of me in my mortar board and gown with my proud parents and now I had as near as I will ever get.

The CIMA Award

I got some recognition for my studies too. One of my **LinkedIn** followers, I'll call **Sam**, reached out to me. I had never spoken to her before. She sent me the following message, **"Hi Gavin, I've been following your posts for a while. You're doing a great job of raising awareness of what's possible while you've been qualifying so I wondered if you had considered the awards so I thought I'd forward this on."** Attached was an advert looking for nominations for **Student Of The Year** for **CIMA's** annual awards. I sent the following reply:

Gavin Simpson ACMA CGMA • 11:23 AM

[redacted]

I did have a look and to be honest, looking through the categories and the nomination descriptions I didn't think I'd qualify for any of them.

I'd love to be nominated, not for me and my ego but to use it to inform and inspire others. It would really help the cause.

If you feel I do fit in a category I'd be honoured to be nominated if you or anyone else would like to nominate me. I would also feel uncomfortable nominating myself for an award.

Thank you for thinking of me, it really means a lot.

Sam replied straight back with the following message:

[redacted] (She/Her) • 12:23 PM

Hi Gavin

I think as a professional body we need to be raising the voices of people like yourself where others can see what's possible.

I struggled to pass dome of my exams and I remember all of the accolades for the highest scoring students and wondering where that left me so although my journey is a little different to yours I do recognise what it's like to come from a place where you either think it might not be possible or you might not fit in.

I can understand why you would found it difficult to nominate yourself but I would like to put your name forward as you really stand out as someone who embodies where I think the profession shpuld be going in the future.

I'll have a look at the nomination form and keep you posted 🙂

I just still didn't see myself as worthy and replied with the following:

> Thank you [redacted]
>
> To be honest reading the nomination descriptions it made me feel a little worthless like I did at school. It's all about the high achievers. I think that kind of thought hinders the profession and industry as you don't celebrate diversity and include the people that can problem solve and think outside the box.
>
> Being neurodivergent we have spiky profiles, we excel at some things and not others so many will never shine in an academic world.
>
> It's like having a stack of Xbox and playstation games mixed together and trying to play them all on a playstation. Many you will disregard as being no good as they work on a different system, society and the current system sees them as no good, yet in the right environment they can be just as good, if not better!
>
> Thank you again [redacted]

Sam wasn't prepared to give up though and asked if she could nominate me. I agreed. ***What was the harm? It wasn't like I was going to win.***

A couple of months later, I was contacted by CIMA. I had been nominated and in fact **short-listed** and invited to a posh ceremony at the Hilton Hotel, Tower Bridge, London, in the shadows of the mighty Shard. I truly couldn't believe it. Kerry and I were so excited. I informed Sam. She was so happy for me. I told my Dad. He was bursting with pride. I told my kids. They didn't get it. Oliver, by this time, hated me talking about **Neurodiversity** and would roll his eyes.

I'm sure that one day he will read this book and be proud. **Oliver, you are my inspiration!**

In **October of 2024**, we headed to London. It was a rare opportunity to spend some time together; we hardly ever had child care. I treated us to a room, not in The Hilton, we still couldn't afford that, but in a hotel just on the other side of the river—a room with a view, a room right next to the river Thames and right next to Tower Bridge. The view was immense. With the bridge lit up in the evening, it was so magical. We dressed ourselves up—Kerry in a beautiful navy dress, me in a navy suit and matching tie—and nervously headed off. We walked into a champagne reception. I felt nervous and out of place. I didn't know anyone. Kerry and I huddled together at a table sipping our champagne nervously. We had some lovely people approach us and talk, and we started to settle.

We went to the function room, found our name cards, and sat down. The compere for the evening was none other than the magician Ben Hanlin. We had the most amazing **three-course** meal. It was a far cry from a bacon roll on an industrial estate sat in a truck that had been carting around sewage. Ben Hanlin did some amazing magic and entertained us. He was great.

Then came the moment. I had created a speech, as I had been asked to. I never thought I would need it. Ben read out the category and it was announced that this winner had overcome immense barriers during their studies, battled on with grit and determination, dealt with **Neurodiversity**, and had smashed the class ceiling. *Oh, there is someone else that has done this* I thought, *or could it be?* **And the winner is…Gavin Simpson.**

I welled up. In fact, I'm welling up now just reliving the moment. This useless boy that would amount to nothing was here, in his suit at the prestigious **Hilton Hotel**, in the heart of London, winning an award for being the best at something. This was immense! I walked to the stage. I had forgotten about my penguin walk. I just waddled on to the stage, overwhelmed with happiness, the lights flashing, and **"Mr Brightside" by The Killers** was blaring out of the speakers. Ben Hanlin and the **CIMA President** shook my hand, and I was invited to the podium for my speech.

I had it written and in my suit pocket, but my hands were shaking and I was so overwhelmed. I just said it from the heart.

"Wow, wow, I'm just a little bit gobsmacked. Firstly, I just wanted to say thank you to my wife, Kerry. I have done this while we have brought up three children all with special needs as well as having a full-time job, so doing this has been quite a journey. Ten years ago, I was driving a dustcart for a living and had no qualifications, and now I'm a Finance Business Partner for [name redacted]. I want to try and use this [holding up the award] to show that there is so much hidden talent out there." I tried to continue, but it was so emotional. My voice started going, and the whole room burst out in applause. "Mr Brightside" from The Killers played again. Ben shook my hand and told me how inspiring my speech was.

I headed back to the table, on top of the world, my smile filling my whole face. I don't think I could have generated a bigger smile if I'd tried. Kerry flung her arms around me. **"I love you. I am so proud of you."** I tried so hard to hold back the tears. The years of pain, of torture, of being told I was useless and would amount to nothing, **I had just proved them all wrong!** People came up to me telling me I had made them cry and how amazing my speech was. So many people wanted to speak to me that evening, I actually finally felt worthy of being there.

I promised that evening that **I would try to make a difference, and I will. I will not give up the fight. I will leave this world having made a difference, I assure you. I won't rest until I have.**

The Final Word on Mrs. Cooper

As we get to the end of this section of the book, I would like to share with you one final story. Remember **Mrs. Cooper**? Well, I used **Facebook** for one good thing. I found a group that was dedicated to memories of the school around the time I was there. I mentioned I was writing this book and I had fond memories of Mrs. Cooper. She had given me hope, a little ray of light that I was good at something. I had a reply, from none other than **Mrs. Jane Cooper**—wow! We spoke on chat and arranged to meet for lunch. After over **30 years**, we were going to meet, me and Mrs. Cooper.

The day came. I was there early, excited but nervous, and in came Mrs. Cooper. I could tell it was her in an instant. I wasn't a hugger, but our arms flew out, and we hugged. It was so amazing.

We spoke non stop for over **three hours**; the time just flew by. What amazed me most is that **Jane** had remembered me all of these years. She remembered my love of fishing, and she remembered that she had told me that I should think of another route, that my dream wasn't possible. Jane also remembered that chance meeting in **Sainsbury's** where I told her I was living my dream working for an **Ex-World Champion** fisherman. Jane explained that she had told many children about me after that day and that it had changed her mind. From that point on, she had **encouraged every child to chase their dreams.**

Jane, Mrs. Cooper, you are amazing, but I have one last thing to ask you as my teacher, please Miss, can you mark my work one last time?

Gavin, would be delighted to!

Gavin's story is inspiring, proving how sheer determination can overcome the most challenging of circumstances but also highlighting the need for significant change in our education system and in wider society's appreciation of the strengths of the neurodivergent.

In 40 years of teaching, I have taught thousands of students. Sadly, not being gifted with the best of memories, I have forgotten far more of them than I have remembered. So how is it that, as soon as I received messages that Gavin was trying to track me down, I knew who he was, more than 40 years later?

Well, somehow, I had never forgotten the quirky boy who had proudly showed me a picture of himself in a camouflage bucket hat holding a prize winning catch. Nor had I forgotten the lesson he had taught me: never tell a student their dream is unrealistic. I had often used Gavin as an example in assemblies, encouraging young people to pursue their dream—albeit whilst having a back up plan just in case.

For all Gavin's kind words about me, I am only too well aware that there will have been very many neurodivergent students whom I failed to understand and support, back then and even today. In the 90's neurodivergence wasn't even a topic in teacher training and my only awareness of Autism would have come from watching the film Rain Man. So my connection with Gavin didn't stem from intellectual knowledge, but rather the fact that we could discuss fishing! I had spent countless hours as a child and a young teenager fishing with my Dad so I was genuinely interested in Gavin's passion. Had his obsession been with football, I doubt such a connection would have been formed!

Gavin's journey has been remarkable and the end of this book is just the start of the next stage of that journey. The message Gavin gives us about the education system forcing square pegs into round holes and the need for businesses to recognise the untapped potential of many employees is vital. Unfortunately, with some of my current students having to wait 3-4 years for a diagnosis, the wheels of change are moving far too slowly. If this book and the accompanying website (EDIT: www.binmantoboardroom.com), can help to drive forward that change, then my quirky student in the camouflage hat will have achieved far more than any of his teachers could ever have envisaged.

Jane.

Thank you Jane, I really appreciate your hard work in helping me edit this book and the best thing I have got out of this is a fantastic friendship as I have enjoyed our chats over lunch immensely and hope that they will continue for many years to come.

You showed interest in me, believed in me when others didn't and left me with a feeling that I might one day achieve something despite the negative experience I had of school overall. Without that I doubt this book would even exist, you have always given me hope and I have never forgotten that hope you gave me, I have mentioned you countless times over the years.

During our time catching up we have spoken many times about the education system and I asked Jane if she could answer the following two questions for me to publish in this book.

Do you feel that further changes are needed in the way children are taught in the UK, especially now we are learning more about neurotypes?

Yes, specifically we need more teaching assistants to provide in class support. Smaller class sizes would also help. I'd like to add, 'Sadly, academisation is driving an agenda of conformity rather than individuality.

Do you feel that the training teachers receive, in general, around Neurodiversity is sufficient?

No - it's still not a big enough part of our continuing professional development. As with everything, there is never enough time! Teachers are expected to be educators, social workers, guardians of morality, counsellors and psychologists. All while teaching classes of 30 plus which may contain a wide range of abilities, learning styles and neurodiversities. We are only human. Far more investment is needed in the education system.

So let's think about this, if students, parents, teachers, professionals, and organisations all advocate for change, why is it not happening? The core issue is funding. However, my business acumen has shown me that economy does not always equate to efficiency or effectiveness. We are also neglecting to see the bigger picture. While Special Educational Needs (SEN) reform and modernising our outdated education system will undoubtedly require investment, the subsequent section will highlight the significant cost of inaction and how a revised strategy could save the UK tens of billions.

My unwavering purpose is to push for this necessary change. We all need it—businesses need it—to foster future talent that is empowered, not disheartened, enabled and not held back. I urge you to share this book and its message with others. Let us collaborate to build a better world for our children.

Thank you.

Gavin Simpson ACMA CGMA
Thank you for purchasing and reading my book. I hope it has been both helpful and insightful. It brings me great pleasure to help others, so please feel free to contact me and let me know if the book has achieved this for you. I have new exciting journeys ahead and at the time of this being in its final stages I have become the founder and director of two limited companies.

Neuvantage Business Service Limited is a Chartered Accountancy practice, a practice that thinks differently and offers businesses a co-pilot service, giving them direction and moving them forwards, not just reporting on what had happened. You can find out more at www.neuvantage.com.

Binman To Boardroom Limited is based around this book, and future books I have already started writing, including a complete framework of how I turned my life around and how you can too! My website www.binmantoboardroom.com offers free resources to help you on YOUR personal journey and will also come to offer courses including one 2 one and group live sessions. I am also available for keynote and public speaking too, all contact details are on my website.

If you would like to follow the next stage of my exciting journey please do join the mailing list on my website and like, follow and subscribe to my numerous social channels, all of which are listed at the top of my websites.

Goodbye for now, be you, always!

Gavin.

Part 2 - A Further Understanding

Introduction

I wanted this book to be not just about me but also **informative**, a book of reference and learning. Therefore, I decided I would write a separate section for you to come back to for reference. Perhaps you aren't hugely interested in the details of my personal journey and may want to just learn more about **neurodiversity** and **social mobility**.

This is my guide and reference for you, designed to arm you with the knowledge to create better environments, whether that's in the classroom, the boardroom, or at home.

Chapter 1 - Neurodiversity, What Is It?

Before I start this chapter, it's essential to point out that I have no formal training in this area. My knowledge is built entirely from **lived experience**—from reading countless books, navigating diagnoses with my children, and finally, being diagnosed myself. This book is based on my views and experience, backed up by statistics from experts in the field.

Defining Neurodivergence: A Natural Variation

The concept starts with the whole population. The term **neurodiversity** was first used by the Australian Sociologist **Judy Singer** in the 1990s, who is **Neurodivergent** herself. It is a concept used to describe the entire human population, asserting that differences in brain function are normal and natural. Every one of us is unique, made up of how our brains are wired and the journey and experiences we've had in life.

The majority of people—thought to be around **80%** of the population, or four out of five—have a brain that follows the most common structure. This is called **Neurotypical**, and society, schools, and workplaces are largely aligned to this brain type. In contrast, approximately **20%** of the population have a brain that is wired differently: this is **Neurodivergent**. This one-in-five statistic is crucial for leaders and teachers to remember. If you teach a class of 30 children, **six of your pupils** may learn differently, and you may not even know it. If you manage a large organization of 40,000 colleagues, you could have **8,000 Neurodivergent** employees. Getting the environment right for them is the key to unlocking massive potential.

The brain working differently is not a negative thing. Think of it this way: Is an **Apple** phone inherently better than an **Android**? They both do the same thing and are fantastic at what they do. One may excel at specific tasks the other doesn't. The problem arises when you try to run a PlayStation game on an Xbox—it just doesn't work. This highlights why so many **Neurodivergent** people struggle or are out of work. In fact, only **33%** of Autistic people are in full-time employment, largely because the environments they encounter are wrong.

Why We Prefer "Neurodivergent"

You'll notice that most diagnostic labels contain prefixes like *'dis'* or *'dys'* (such as 'disorder'), which have very negative connotations. Because of this, many people now prefer the umbrella term **Neurodivergent**—it is not as downgrading as those conditions named years ago when understanding was limited. This umbrella term also covers conditions that often overlap, such as **ADHD** and **Autism**, which many call **AuDHD**.

Over the years, many of these conditions have also been termed **learning disabilities**. My aim is to change this narrative. **Neurodiversity is not a disability to learn; it is a sensitivity to environments.** If the right environment and equity are provided, there is no disability to learn. However, we must always be mindful that some **Neurodivergent** people may also have genuine intellectual disabilities. Finally, remember: **Neurodiversity** and **Mental Health** are two totally separate things, though statistics show **90%** of **Neurodivergent** people will struggle with their mental health at some point.

The Core Neurodivergent Conditions

Please bear in mind, **no two people will ever be the same**. Every **Neurodivergent** person is unique. There will also be many common crossovers.

Autism Spectrum Disorder (ASD)

The term *Autism* was first used in 1908 by Psychiatrist **Eugen Leuler** and comes from the Greek word *autós* (self). The **Autism Spectrum** is enormous. It includes nonverbal individuals who are highly intelligent, like **Elizabeth Bonker** (who runs a global business), and people who have learned to blend in (**masking**), like myself, and famous figures **Sir Anthony Hopkins** and **Chris Packham**.

My own traits illustrate the complexity: I am very **introverted** (socializing is draining) and struggle with **sensory issues** (noise, sharp points, textures). Conversely, my strengths are immense **problem-solving**, incredible **visualization skills** (the CAD brain I used to build the playhouse), and intense **hyperfocus** that drove my passions. The **UK Government** currently reports that around **1 in 100** of us are Autistic, though the true number is much higher, at potentially **1.2 million**.

Attention Deficit Hyperactivity Disorder (ADHD)

ADHD is a change in brain function that often results in a chaotic and unorganised mind. This makes it hard to focus, difficult to sit still, and leads to impulsivity and forgetfulness. The struggle to deal with perceived criticism can manifest as **RSD (Rejection Sensitivity Dysphoria)**—the physical pain I described that feels like a vice crushing my head.

The positive flip side is extraordinary **creativity**, **boundless energy**, and **hyperfocus**. This intense focus is what fuelled my passions for fishing, music, and eventually, finance, making it a gift when placed in the right environment. Famous figures include **Michael Phelps**, **Jim Carey**, and **Paris Hilton**.

Dyslexia

The word **Dyslexia** comes from the German *dys* (difficult) and the Greek *lexis* (speech/word), and was once known as **Word Blindness**. While many associate it with just poor spelling, it actually changes the way the brain sees words, sometimes making them appear to move across the page. The positive side of **Dyslexia** is often exceptional **problem-solving** and the ability to **visualize in 3D**, much like the exploded view images of an engine I loved in a **Haynes Manual**. It's no surprise that many famous entrepreneurs are **Dyslexic**, including **Richard Branson** and **Ingvar Kamprad**, the founder of **IKEA**.

Tourette's Syndrome (TS)

Tourette's Syndrome (TS) is a neurological condition characterised by involuntary movements and sounds called **tics**. Tics are involuntary, repetitive movements and vocalisations. However, the media often only portrays the most extreme form: **coprolalia** (involuntary swearing).

In reality, most tics are mild, common forms are eye blinking, coughing, throat clearing, or repeating words and phrases. Like other **Neurodivergent** conditions, tics are often exacerbated by **stress** and **anxiety**, meaning a toxic environment will make a person's struggles more visible and pronounced. While there is no known positive trait, many individuals with Tourette's often show high levels of **verbal intelligence**, **creativity**, and **attention to detail**, especially in controlled, supportive environments. Famous figures include singer **Billie Eilish** and former professional footballer **Tim Howard**.

The Broader Neurodivergent Umbrella

The four conditions above are the most commonly discussed, but the umbrella of **Neurodiversity** is wide and ever-growing. There are many other conditions that affect how people process information, learn, and interact.

- **Dyspraxia** (also known as Developmental Coordination Disorder or DCD): Affects physical coordination, balance, and motor skills (the struggles I saw on the balance beam on sports day and mine in my school days too).

- **Dyscalculia**: Affects the ability to acquire arithmetical skills and understand numbers.
- **Dysgraphia**: Affects writing abilities, fine motor skills, and translating thoughts into written words (my own struggles with hand cramps and my son's challenges with writing).

Chapter 2 - The Spiky Profile Hall of Fame: A Different Kind of Genius

I've spent a lot of time thinking about what it means to be different. The countless hours alone, poring over fishing tackle catalogues, or the intense focus I'd have on my model cars, lining them up by colour and shade. For years, I just thought I was a weird kid, a quiet kid—a kid that just didn't get it. I bet a lot of you reading this feel the same way. Maybe you've been told you're too intense, too sensitive, or just too much.

It wasn't until I started to look into **neurodiversity** that I had my "AHA" moment. I realised that my quirks weren't flaws—they were clues. And I started to see these clues everywhere, in the lives of the people who built the world we live in. The artists, the musicians, the inventors. It wasn't merely that they were "smart"; they were inherently **wired differently**.

What is the Spiky Profile?

The **Spiky Profile** is the best visual representation of a **Neurodivergent** mind. Society, schools, and workplaces expect people to have a **"flat profile"**—meaning you score at least average across all skills, from maths and reading to social cues and memory.

However, a **spiky profile** is characterised by possessing **towering peaks of exceptional strength** alongside **deep valleys of significant weakness**. For example, a person might have world-class pattern recognition (a peak) but struggle profoundly with auditory processing or making eye contact (a valley).

My personal experience is a perfect example of this: I could master complex logistical and financial systems (**Peaks**), but a noisy office or an unexpected meeting (a social/sensory **Valley**) could trigger a full physical shutdown. The people in this chapter succeeded because they found an environment that rewarded their peaks while allowing them to manage or circumvent their valleys.

This is the proof that the things you've been told were your greatest weaknesses are actually your most powerful strengths.

The Innovators: Building a World on a Different Foundation

You think of an inventor or an entrepreneur, and you probably imagine some perfectly polished genius with a flawless plan. That's not how it works. The greatest innovators didn't follow the script; they tore it up and wrote their own. They didn't see the world like everyone else. And that difference is what made them successful.

Albert Einstein: The Power of the Imaginary

Albert Einstein is the classic **spiky profile**. He didn't speak until he was around three years old, and he struggled with the traditional school system. His grades in subjects like history and languages were often poor, and one of his teachers famously told him that **"nothing would ever come of him."** He had a hard time with rote memorisation and language, but he had an incredible mind for physics and maths.

His spiky profile wasn't just a weakness in the classroom; it was the foundation of his greatest strength: **visualisation**. He couldn't just learn a formula; he had to *see* it in his mind. He would imagine himself riding on a beam of light. This unique way of thinking is what led him to the theory of relativity.

He said it himself: **"I have no special talent. I am only passionately curious."** It wasn't about being the smartest; it was about asking the questions no one else thought to ask. Albert Einstein was the absolute epitome of the **'5 Whys'** we use in business. Albert had a saying that if he had an hour to solve a problem, he would spend 55 minutes thinking about the problem and 5 minutes on the solution.

Isambard Kingdom Brunel: The Visionary in the Details

Brunel, the man who built the Great Western Railway, was a force of nature, known for his **obsessive attention to detail** and his ability to **visualise a project from start to finish**.

His **spiky profile** was a tireless, almost **manic focus** on every single aspect of a project. The Great Western Railway was so perfect because of the relentless, **"neurodivergent" mind** that saw a straight line from London to Bristol, even when others said it was impossible.

Richard Branson: The Relentless Entrepreneur

Richard Branson famously left school at 16 with no qualifications. Why? Because Branson has **Dyslexia**. He struggled with reading and writing, and the traditional classroom was a nightmare for him. He was a perfect example of a **"rose in the desert"**—a mind with incredible potential in an environment that was killing it.

He said, **"My dyslexia has shaped the way I run my business. It's given me the freedom to think in a different way."** Because he couldn't get bogged down in details and small print, he was forced to learn to be a master delegator. What was a disadvantage in one environment became his "unfair advantage" in another.

Ingvar Kamprad: The IKEA Genius

Ingvar Kamprad, the founder of **IKEA**, struggled with **Dyslexia**. In a business world that demands perfect, polished written communication, he struggled with remembering product numbers. His solution? He invented a system, giving his products simple, memorable names instead of complex codes. **He changed the system to fit his brain.**

The Technology Mavericks: Rewriting the Rules

In the world of technology, a different way of thinking isn't a bonus; it's a necessity.

Bill Gates: The Dropout Who Started a Revolution

Bill Gates, the founder of **Microsoft**, famously dropped out of Harvard. His mind was so **intensely focused** on the problem of personal computing that the traditional academic environment couldn't contain him. He had a singular, relentless focus that many would now identify as a hallmark of a **spiky profile**.

He said, **"I never took a day off in my twenties. Not one."** That's a mind driven by a singular, **obsessive purpose**.

Steve Jobs: The Perfectionist Outsider

Steve Jobs, the co-founder of **Apple**, was a ruthless perfectionist with an intense, often socially difficult, focus on his vision. His **spiky profile** was his insistence that things be done a certain way, his incredible ability to **hyper-focus on design**, and his unwavering belief in the power of simplicity.

The Artists & Entertainers: Seeing a World Others Couldn't

Artists are often seen as eccentric. The truth is, many of the greatest artists were simply seeing the world in a different way. Their art was often a **necessary form of communication** for minds that struggled with social norms and the spoken word.

Dame Gillian Lynne: The Rose in the Desert

This story, right here, is the very heart of this book. You remember how I talked about the rose that won't grow in the desert? Well, this is the story that proves it.

Dame Gillian Lynne, the choreographer of *Cats* and *The Phantom of the Opera*, was a little girl in the 1940s who couldn't sit still in a classroom. A doctor listened, saw her passion in movement, and told her mother: **"She's not naughty; she's a dancer. Send her to a dance school."** Her success came from finding the **right environment to bloom**.

Vincent van Gogh: The Fire Inside

Vincent van Gogh's life was a struggle, filled with intense mental distress. His **spiky profile** meant he experienced the world in an overwhelming, visceral way. He felt things more deeply, saw colours more intensely, and struggled to filter the **sensory overload**. His art was a way to translate that truth.

Jamie Oliver: The Culinary Revolutionary

Jamie Oliver will be the first to tell you that school was a battle due to his **Dyslexia**. But while the other kids were memorising dates, Jamie was learning with his hands and his senses. He found his "right environment" in the kitchen.

He said, **"My dyslexia made me who I am. It made me more creative, and it gave me a better palate."** This is a man who turned his "weakness" into a global brand.

The Mavericks: Finding Your Place in a World Not Built for You

These are the people who have taken their **spiky profiles** and turned them into a public force, using their platform to help others understand themselves.

Guy Martin: The Relentless Engineer and Racer

Guy Martin, the motorcycle racer, spoke about his **Asperger's syndrome** diagnosis, he also referred to the diagnosis as a **"load of tripe"**. His **intense focus**, need for order, and meticulous attention to detail are not weaknesses for an engineer or a racer—they are the very things that have made him so successful.

Chris Packham: The Unfiltered Voice of Nature

Chris Packham has spoken candidly about his **Autism**. His spiky profile—the **intense focus** and the **unfiltered honesty**—is what makes him such a brilliant and trusted voice on television.

Anne Hegerty: The Quiz Master

Anne Hegerty (The Governess) is open about her **Autism** diagnosis. Her spiky profile gives her an incredible ability to **focus and recall information**—a superpower that finds its perfect home in the rigid, rule-based world of a quiz show.

Greta Thunberg: The Unfiltered Voice

Greta Thunberg has publicly stated that her **Autism** is her superpower. Her diagnosis means she doesn't see things in shades of grey; she sees the truth. Her **unwavering, logical voice** cuts through the noise. As she put it: **"Being different is not an illness. It is a gift."**

Your Spiky Profile

Every one of these people had a **spiky profile** that was once seen as a problem. They were told they were slow, or odd, or too intense. But they all found a way to take the things that made them different and turn them into the very thing that made them great.

Your struggle isn't a sign that you're broken. It's a sign that you have a **unique way of seeing the world**. A mind that's built for a different purpose. It's time to stop looking down at that black hole of emptiness and start looking up at the sky.

The world is waiting for your genius.

To find out more about YOUR spiky profile, scan the QR code below

Chapter 3 - It's Not a Trend: The Truth About a Changing World

I've heard it countless times. On the news, in pub conversations, even from some well-meaning people in my life: **"Autism and ADHD are just a trend. Everyone's getting diagnosed now."**

Every time I hear it, I want to scream. It's an ignorant, dangerous lie that dismisses the genuine struggles of millions of people. It's a lie that completely ignores the undeniable fact that the world we live in is a very different place from the one my grandad lived in, or even the one I grew up in.

The truth is, **neurodivergent** people haven't changed. The world has. And the diagnostic process has changed.

This chapter is the evidence. This is the truth, backed by the history of diagnosis and a deep understanding of what it means to be a **spiky profile** in a flat-line world that's getting brighter, faster, and louder by the minute.

My Own Ignorance: The Problem with a One-Dimensional View

Before I started this journey of self-discovery, I was no better than anyone else. My understanding of **Autism** was just a bunch of stereotypes painted by Hollywood. Movies like *Rain Man* gave us Raymond Babbitt, a character with an incredible photographic memory who couldn't handle his own life. Or *Mercury Rising*, where a genius autistic child was a walking, talking government code.

These portrayals created a one-dimensional, and often dehumanising, view of an entire group of people. I believed those stereotypes. It never occurred to me that an **Autistic** person could be someone who struggled through school like me, or someone who worked in a factory like me. It never occurred to me that an **Autistic** person could be a friend, a father, a husband, or a worker just trying to make their way in the world. It’s a powerful lesson in how the lack of a proper, nuanced understanding can cause so much personal pain.

The Family Tree of a Spiky Profile

My family is a living case study of this truth. I have many **neurodivergent** traits. My dad does, too. And when I talk to my family, I hear stories about my grandad and my great-grandad. They were just seen as **"eccentric."** They were a bit "odd."

My great-grandad, for example, didn't like company and spent most of his time alone in his garden. His obsession was plants, and he had an **encyclopaedic knowledge** of them. He wasn't diagnosed with anything. He was just seen as a **"character."** He found his **right environment** in the quiet of his garden.

This is the key. The traits have always been there. In my great-grandad's time, the world was slower, quieter, and more rural. You could be a "character" and still thrive. In today's world, that same person might be a child in a classroom that's a cacophony of noise, with fluorescent lights flickering, and an overwhelming amount of social demands. It's a completely different environment for the same brain.

The History of a Diagnosis: From Misunderstanding to the Spectrum

The term **Autism** didn’t even exist in my great-grandad’s lifetime. And when it did, the understanding of it was incredibly limited. This is a story of a scientific and social awakening.

From Kanner to Asperger: The history of Autism diagnosis is a messy one. It was first described in the 1940s by two separate doctors: **Leo Kanner** and **Hans Asperger**. Kanner focused on severe cases. Asperger, working in Vienna, saw children who were intelligent but struggled socially, had intense interests, and were physically clumsy. He was one of the first people to see the **genius in the spiky profile**, describing their potential for greatness and **"extremely original thought."**

The Problem with Asperger's: For decades, the work was largely ignored. When **"Asperger's Syndrome"** did become a mainstream diagnosis, it created a harmful division between "high-functioning" and "low-functioning" Autism. More importantly, it was later revealed that Hans Asperger was complicit with the **Nazi regime**, sending children he deemed "unfit" to their deaths. Because of this, the diagnosis was removed in 2013 and folded into one single diagnosis: **Autism Spectrum Disorder (ASD)**. This was a huge step forward because it recognised that we are all on a spectrum, and that every person's experience is different.

The Modern World: A Sensory Overload

The world today is a sensory explosion. Think about a normal day. We are constantly bombarded with:

- **Light:** The harsh fluorescent lights in a supermarket, the flickering glare of a screen, the bright lights from a car at night, the constant looking at a mobile phone. For a brain that is sensitive to sensory input, this is a constant source of stress.
- **Noise:** The background hum of an office, the endless traffic on the roads, the cacophony of a busy train station. In my great-grandad's time, there was silence. Now, it is a luxury. For a brain that struggles to filter out background noise, this is a constant, exhausting battle just to think.
- **Information:** We are constantly connected, with information and demands coming at us from all angles. For a **neurodivergent** brain that needs to focus on one thing at a time, this can lead to an immediate and overwhelming sense of paralysis.

This isn't a theory. Research has shown that **sensory sensitivities** are a core part of many **neurodivergent** conditions, including **Autism** and **ADHD**. For a brain that has a hard time filtering out this background noise and sensory input, it's going to be far more likely to suffer from mental health issues, anxiety, and burnout in today's world. The environment has changed, and it's making it harder to be a **spiky profile**.

The Hereditary Factor: A Family Affair

The idea that **neurodiversity** is a "trend" completely ignores the fact that these traits are often passed down through families. It's a genetic lottery.

The Science: Research has consistently shown that **neurodiversity** has a strong genetic component. If a parent is **neurodivergent**, there is a significantly higher chance that their children will be as well. It's what's known as a **polygenic inheritance pattern**, where many different genes combine to increase the likelihood of **neurodivergent** traits.

The Multiplication Effect: The traits have always been there. In my great-grandad's day, he found his quiet garden. Now, the family tree branches out. This is what's known as the **Multiplication Effect** of **polygenic inheritance**. If two parents have a child, one of whom is **neurodivergent**, that child may carry those traits. When that child grows up and marries a partner, whether neurotypical or neurodivergent, they may have **two or three neurodivergent children** of their own. As these children in turn marry and reproduce, the traits branch out exponentially across the family tree, increasing the likelihood that the next generation will express **neurodivergent** conditions. This explains why **neurodiversity has always existed**, but as understanding and diagnostic rates increase, the total number of people receiving a diagnosis grows rapidly with each successive generation.

This isn't a trend; it's just the natural progression of genetics meeting a world that is now asking a different set of questions.

The Future of Neurodiversity: A Fast-Moving Horizon

Our understanding of the brain is moving at a phenomenal pace. When I was a kid, if you had a lot of energy, you were just seen as a "naughty child." Today, we understand that it could be **ADHD** or **Autism**. In my life, a close friend was told he was a poor reader because he was "lazy," when in fact, he was **Dyslexic**. The lack of understanding nearly crushed his genius mind.

The key to all of this is that the knowledge is growing. A lot of people are now receiving a dual diagnosis—being diagnosed with both **Autism** and **ADHD**, which is often called **AuDHD**. This isn't a fad. It's science. It shows that the old, rigid categories were too simple. It proves that a person can have a brain that is both deeply structured and chaotic at the same time.

The truth is, **neurodiversity** has always been here. We've just become better at understanding it, and the world has become harder for it. So, when people tell you it's a "trend," you can smile and tell them the truth: **It's the diagnosis that's on the rise, not the people.**

Below you can find a link to more information

Chapter 4 - The £30 Billion Price Tag: The Cost of a Broken System

All my life, I was told I was a problem. From the fellow students at school who called me a "boffin" to the roofing boss who told me I was "useless." The system, the one-size-fits-all world that we've all been raised in, looks at a **spiky profile** and sees a flaw. It sees a person who is too much of one thing and not enough of another.

But what happens when you turn that problem on its head? What if the problem isn't with the people, but with the system that can't see their genius?

When I became a **Chartered Management Accountant**, I learned to look at the world in a different way. I learned to look at numbers, at the economy, at the cost of a business failing to be efficient. And what I saw broke my heart. I saw a staggering financial price tag attached to the very thing I had lived through my entire life. I saw a system that, by failing to understand and nurture **neurodiversity**, was losing **billions of pounds** of unrealised potential.

This isn't just a human story of struggle. It's a multi-billion-pound financial crisis.

The Human Cost: The Story of Ivan

I worked with a man named **Ivan**. He was in his mid-fifties, a grafter, a quiet man who kept to himself. But Ian had a secret. In his spare time, he created some coding that gave us a massive insight into the business, allowing us to save thousands of pounds. He had a **genius mind** for patterns and logic.

Ivan had a **spiky profile**. He had a brilliant mind, but he had nuances that the world didn't understand. He was seen by management as militant and negative, simply because he cared deeply about the work. They saw a problem to be managed, not a genius to be nurtured.

He died of cancer around a year later, never having realised his dream. **He died as a genius in a warehouse, his untapped potential lost forever to the world.** He is the human cost of a broken system.

The Cost to Society: The Numbers that Prove the Pain

As an accountant, I know that for every human tragedy like Ivan's, there is a financial calculation. The numbers don't lie. They show that by not investing in a system that supports **neurodiversity**, the UK is actively bleeding **billions of pounds**.

The Cost of an Incomplete Talent Pool and the Narrowing Funnel

I've sat in boardrooms and lecture halls and listened to leaders talk about talent acquisition. They talk about skill gaps and the need to find the best and brightest. But what they often don't realise is that they are looking for that talent in all the wrong places.

At this moment, the **UK is going through a massive divide** that is resulting in political pressure to **raise the barriers to foreign talent**. This is limiting the influx of skilled workers that our businesses desperately need. Since we are restricting the external talent pool, we must immediately become better at finding and nurturing our **own home-grown talent**.

However, if our education system and workplaces are still built for the **flat-line brain**, we are actively **narrowing the talent funnel** right here on our doorstep. We are leaving behind a massive pool of untapped genius. This failure risks businesses struggling further as they cannot fill crucial roles. It's not just a social problem; it's a direct threat to **business sustainability**.

The **Centre for Economic Performance** estimates that better support for **neurodivergent** individuals could boost the UK's **GDP** by up to **£30 billion a year**. That is a game-changing amount of money that proves we are wasting our most valuable asset.

The Cost to the Justice System

For a **neurodivergent** person who struggles with social cues or impulse control, the justice system can be a brutal and confusing place. Over **50% of young offenders** in the UK are believed to have some form of learning disability or **neurodivergence**. The cost of keeping a single person in prison is approximately **£40,000 per year**. That's a minimum of **£1 billion a year** just to manage the result of a broken system.

The Cost of a Lost Generation: The Rise of NEETs

The system's failure starts in the classroom. Our education system is still built for the **flat-line brain**. It's a conveyor belt that leaves children with **spiky profiles** behind. This is evidenced by the staggering rise in **NEETs (Not in Education, Employment, or Training)**. Research shows that **neurodivergent** individuals are significantly **overrepresented** in this group. It's not a lack of intelligence; it's a **failure of the system**.

The Cost of Groupthink: How a Lack of Diverse Minds Kills Business

Groupthink is the silent killer of innovation. It's when a team of smart people all think the same way, preventing them from seeing the **"spiky," disruptive ideas** that are waiting to be found.

Case Study: Kodak & the Digital Camera

Kodak invented the first digital camera in 1975, but their leadership—a room full of "flat-liners"—told the inventor to hide it, famously saying: **"That's cute, but don't tell anyone about it."** They were so locked into their existing business model that they couldn't see a future where their product was obsolete. The result? Kodak **filed for bankruptcy in 2012**. Kodak was killed not by a lack of genius, but by a lack of **diverse thought**.

Case Study: Blockbuster & the Streaming Revolution

Blockbuster laughed **Netflix** out of the room when offered a partnership. Blockbuster's lack of a **spiky profile** at the decision-making table meant they couldn't see the future where streaming dominated. Their failure was a **lack of vision**.

The Solution: A New Way of Thinking

My journey—from a binman to a **Chartered Management Accountant**—is living proof that my brain didn't change; the **environment** did. I learned what my strengths were, and I found a place where my **spiky profile** was an asset, not a flaw.

The cost of inaction is too high. The billions are just a number. The Ivans of this world are the true price we're paying. And we can't afford to lose another one.

I would like to end this book with an open letter to the Prime Minister….

An Open Letter to the Prime Minister

Dear Prime Minister,

I am writing this letter not as a politician, or a pundit, but as a man who has lived at both ends of this country's social spectrum. I have been a binman. I have been in a boardroom. I have seen the genius in a warehouse and the complacency in a company that can't see a new future.

I have looked at the numbers, and I can tell you that **we are failing**.

We are failing our children by forcing them through a broken education system that labels brilliant minds as problems. We are failing our businesses by allowing a culture of **groupthink** to kill innovation. And we are failing our economy by ignoring a multi-billion-pound talent pool that is already here, waiting to be unleashed.

The **UK's economic future** depends on our ability to embrace the **spiky profiles** of our people. If we fail to **enable our children** and rebuild the system to support them, businesses will **struggle further** as the talent funnel continues to narrow.

We can't afford to lose another **Ivan**. We can't afford to be another **Kodak**.

The solution is not a new policy. It's a new mindset.

I urge you to read this book and fully understand the issue. I urge you to listen to the people who don't have a voice. I urge you to look at the numbers, and more importantly, to look at the human cost behind them.

Our future depends on it.

Sincerely,

Gavin Simpson ACMA CGMA

Chapter 5 - Resources and Next Steps

This book is a journey, not a destination. Whether you are a business leader, a parent, a teacher, or a **neurodivergent** adult, this chapter provides the essential tools, reading, and contacts to continue your path of self-improvement and advocacy.

1. Essential Reading: Books Mentioned in This Book

These books were instrumental in my journey of self-discovery, from learning to manage my "chimp" to mastering accounting concepts.

- ***The Chimp Paradox* by Steve Peters**: Provides the foundational **mental management model** used by the 2012 Olympic cycling team. It teaches you to manage your emotional "Chimp" and empower your rational "Human" brain (Chapter 18).
- ***How To Win Friends and Influence People* by Dale Carnegie**: A cornerstone text on **emotional intelligence** and interpersonal skills. It contains the quote that inspired my personal transformation: "The greatest discovery of my generation is that a human being can alter his life by altering his attitudes" (Chapter 13).
- ***7 Habits of Highly Effective People* by Stephen Covey**: Focuses on personal and professional effectiveness through aligning habits with values, a key strategy for maintaining focus and drive.
- ***Who Moved My Cheese* by Spencer Johnson**: An insightful book on dealing with unexpected change and managing fear, highly relevant to coping with career setbacks and pivots.
- ***Fish! A Remarkable Way to Boost Morale and Improve Results* by Stephen C. Lundin, Harry Paul, John Christensen**: A business parable that informed my early

management style, focusing on attitude and making the workplace fun and engaging (Chapter 7).

- ***Beginner's Guide to Excel* (Various Publishers)**: The first technical book I bought to bridge the knowledge gap between the factory floor and the office (Chapter 10).
- ***Bookkeeping For Dummies* (Dummies Guide Series)**: Provided the basic building blocks of finance and accounting that made the formal **CIMA** material finally accessible (Chapter 11).
- ***The Economics Book* by DK Publishing**: Helped break down complex economic theories into visual, easy-to-understand concepts, catering to my visualization skills (Chapter 11).
- ***Essentials Of Business Law* by Ewan MacIntyre**: A necessary academic text used to pass the challenging **CIMA** Law exams (Chapter 11).
- ***Lawyers' Latin* by John Gray**: Helped decipher the complex Latin phrases required for the Business Law component of my accounting qualification (Chapter 11).
- ***An Introduction To SQL* (Various Publishers)**: The 1,000-page book that fuelled my data obsession and taught me the technical language needed to create multi-million-pound business solutions (Chapter 13).
- ***The Inner Game of Music* by Barry Green and W. Timothy Gallwey**: The first self-help book I read, which explained the internal struggle and the **negative inner voice**—the "Chimp"—long before I had the language for neurodiversity (Chapter 8).

2. Neurodiversity and Disability Organisations (UK Focus)

These organisations are crucial for parents, teachers, and adults seeking support, diagnosis, or advocating for change in the workplace.

- **The National Autistic Society (NAS)**: The leading UK charity for **autistic** people and their families. Provides information, support, and campaigns for better public understanding and services.

- **ADHD UK**: A dedicated charity focused solely on **Attention Deficit Hyperactivity Disorder (ADHD)**. Provides resources, guidance, and community support for those diagnosed and awaiting diagnosis.
- **British Dyslexia Association (BDA)**: A national voice for **dyslexic** people, campaigning for change and providing high-quality training, advice, and information.
- **Dyspraxia Foundation**: Supports individuals and families affected by **Dyspraxia** (Developmental Coordination Disorder), promoting greater understanding and awareness.
- **Tourette's Action**: The UK charity working to support people with **Tourette's Syndrome** and their families.
- **Genius Within**: The specialist business that provided my **Access To Work** coaching (Chapter 17). They help **neurodivergent** individuals maximize their potential and train businesses on how to create inclusive environments.
- **Neurodiversity in Business (NiB)**: The charity I volunteered for (Chapter 17), aimed at transforming corporate culture and encouraging businesses to attract, engage, and retain **neurodivergent** talent.
- **Access to Work (ATW)**: A **government grant scheme** that provides funding for equipment, support workers, and coaching to help disabled people (including **neurodivergent** people) start or stay in work (Chapter 17).

3. Mental Health and Crisis Contacts (UK Emergency)

If you are struggling with a mental health crisis, please remember that you are **not alone**. There are people who care and who want to help.

- **Emergency Services**: **Call 999** or **111** if you feel you are in immediate danger or if you need urgent medical help but it's not life-threatening.
- **Samaritans**: A confidential service available **24/7** for anyone experiencing distress or suicidal thoughts.

- **The Mental Health Foundation**: Provides advice and support to empower anyone experiencing a mental health problem.
- **MIND (National Association for Mental Health)**: Provides advice and support to empower anyone experiencing a mental health problem
- **CALM (Campaign Against Living Miserably)**: A movement against suicide, specifically for men, who are often reluctant to seek help. Offers a daily helpline and webchat.

Thank you for reading my book. I hope to have helped you and others around you. To read more, discover courses or book me as a keynote speaker please, scan the QR code below.